The Limits of Obligation

Russell Hardin Collective Action (Johns Hopkins)
(p. 133)

The Limits of Obligation

James S. Fishkin

NEW HAVEN AND LONDON
Yale University Press

Published with assistance from the
Louis Stern Memorial Fund.

Designed by James J. Johnson
and set in Melior Roman type.
Printed in the United States of America by
Vail-Ballou Press, Binghamton, N.Y.

Library of Congress Cataloging in Publication Data

Fishkin, James S.
    The limits of obligation.

    Includes index.
    1. Ethics.   2. Social ethics.   I. Title.
BJ1012.F54   170   81–13046
ISBN 0–300–02747–8   AACR2
0–300–03078–9 (pbk.)

10   9   8   7   6   5   4   3   2

Contents

Acknowledgments

A first draft of this book was written during part of a Junior Faculty Fellowship awarded by Yale University. Portions of part I were presented as a Cooper Foundation Lecture at Swarthmore College in the fall of 1980. The manuscript was completed during part of a semester's leave supported by a research grant from the National Endowment for the Humanities. Portions of another leave, at the Woodrow Wilson International Center for Scholars in Washington, were devoted to revisions. All of this support is gratefully acknowledged.

The Institution for Social and Policy Studies at Yale and its director, Charles E. Lindblom, provided a stimulating atmosphere for writing this book. I am grateful for this assistance.

The latter sections of part II had an earlier incarnation as part of my Ph.D. thesis in philosophy submitted to the University of Cambridge in January 1976. I would especially like to thank Bernard Williams, my dissertation supervisor. Through his skill and patience over several years, he taught me what philosophy—and teaching—are both about.

My examiners, Derek Parfit and J. E. J. Altham, made many useful comments. In addition, I want to thank Peter Laslett for several discussions and for an early essay, "The Face to Face Society" (*Philosophy, Politics and Society*, First Series), which first drew my attention to problems of social scale.

Several colleagues and friends have also provided helpful comments on the manuscript. I would like to thank Bruce

Ackerman, Charles Beitz, Robert Dahl, Richard Flathman, William Galston, Charles E. Lindblom, Douglas Rae, and Adina Schwartz.

My wife, Shelley, and my father-in-law, Milton Fisher, provided crucial help and support. Several of the best examples in the book are, in fact, theirs.

Last, I owe a crucial debt of thanks to Brian Barry. My conversations with him delayed publication of this work by several years and have, I believe, improved it immeasurably in the end.

PART I:

The General Problem

1. Introduction

We are small individuals in a large world. This fact, so obvious as hardly to require explicit statement, has far-reaching implications for morality. Our common ethical assumptions, which work well at the small scale, break down when they are applied to large enough numbers. In such cases, moral assumptions that seem to be nothing more than common sense lead us to confusion. For this reason, the ethics of individual responsibility and obligation will have to be reassessed in its fundamentals if it is to apply to large-scale social problems.

Let me begin with an example. Although it is one that I find especially disturbing, it is but a particular instance of a more general class of cases that can arise only at the large scale. We would normally assume that if we can save a human life at minor cost, we are obligated to do so. While there is considerable room for discussion about the extent of our obligations for cases of greater risk or sacrifice, the obligation is difficult to deny when the costs of an individual act are clearly insignificant. Let us call this assumption the principle of *minimal altruism*.

But if we apply even so weak a principle as this to some of the opportunities for inexpensive beneficence now available to the citizens of the western developed countries, we will find ourselves obligated to assume enormous burdens. We will, in fact, find ourselves arriving, step by step, at the point where we are obligated to be heroic.

Let us suppose that each small contribution to famine relief, say five or ten dollars, will save another human life by facilitating the delivery of surplus foodstuffs to starving refugees. If we take such charitable appeals seriously, then our principle of minimal altruism requires that we give not only five or ten dollars but many more as well, for each additional small contribution would save another human life at minor cost. Peter Singer, in fact, argues from a principle similar to minimal altruism to an extreme conclusion, namely, that "we ought to give until we reach the level of marginal utility—that is, the level at which, by giving more, I would cause as much suffering to myself or my dependents as I would relieve by my gift. This would mean, of course that one would reduce oneself to very near the material circumstances of a Bengali refugee."[1] Singer modifies this conclusion only to take account of the fact that too great a sacrifice might lessen one's ability to contribute. Hence:

> Strictly, we would need to cut down to the minimum level compatible with earning the income which, after providing for our needs, left us most to give away. Thus if my present position earns me, say, £10,000 a year, but requires me to spend £1,000 a year on dressing respectably and maintaining a car, I cannot save more people by giving away the car and clothes if that will mean taking a job which, although it does not involve me in these expenses, earns me only £5,000.[2]

Note that Singer is arguing that we are *required* to make these enormous sacrifices as a matter of duty or obligation. Giving this much to famine relief is not, on his account, a

---

1. Peter Singer, "Famine, Affluence and Morality," in Peter Laslett and James Fishkin, eds., *Philosophy, Politics and Society*, Fifth Series (Oxford: Basil Blackwell/New Haven: Yale University Press, 1979), pp. 21–35. The quotation is from p. 33. These extreme results follow from the "strong" version of Singer's principle and, as he makes clear later on the same page, he is advocating the strong version.

2. Peter Singer, *Practical Ethics* (Cambridge: Cambridge University Press, 1979), p. 163.

discretionary matter to be thought of as "charity."[3] If we fail to live up to these demands, we are morally blameworthy. His claim is not merely that it would be good to give this much to famine relief, it is also that it would be wrong not to.

I believe that one reason we find Singer's extremely demanding conclusions troubling is that we commonly approach this kind of problem with another assumption, whose application to this problem Singer rejects.[4] This is the assumption that some levels of sacrifice or risk must be heroic or "beyond the call of duty." Let us call this assumption the cutoff for heroism. And we would normally assume that heroism is supererogatory, not obligatory. It is the kind of exemplary behavior that embodies exceptional virtue. The hero has not merely done his duty; he has gone beyond what can be morally demanded or required. And heroic behavior is, in that sense, morally discretionary; we cannot be blamed for failing to live up to such standards, although we can be praised if we manage to succeed in doing so.

Because we commonly assume such a cutoff for heroism, Singer's conclusion is theoretically perplexing as well as morally disturbing. For by definition, we cannot be obligated or required to perform acts that are also supererogatory. We cannot be morally required to be heroes. Yet this kind of case seems to lead us inexorably to that conclusion. For if I gave, say, half my income to famine relief, it would still be the case that five more dollars would be a minor sacrifice. Yet, I believe

---

3. Singer, "Famine, Affluence and Morality," pp. 27–28.

4. Singer considers the possibility of admissible limits on contributions for strategic reasons but not for independent moral ones. Perhaps it is the case that "in order to do the maximum to reduce absolute poverty, we should advocate a standard lower than the amount we think people ought to give." Advocating too much may be "counterproductive." But a cutoff for heroism to be valued for its own sake, and not for such instrumental reasons, is not an assumption he is willing to admit, at least at levels low enough to affect this problem. See his Practical Ethics, pp. 180–81. Perhaps an even greater sacrifice, such as giving up one's life, would be considered supererogatory. But the main point of his essay is that extreme sacrifice at the levels envisioned in the famine-relief argument should not be.

that if I went so far as to give half my income to famine relief, I would not have merely done my duty. Giving half my income would be a supererogatory pattern of conduct. By the cutoff for heroism, it should be considered beyond the call of duty. The difficulty here is that the seemingly innocent assumption of only minimal altruism has led us, incrementally, to the point where we find ourselves *required* to assume such an enormous burden.

This implication follows even when the good accomplished is only temporary. For example, if "twelve dollars will feed a mother and two children for a week" (who are otherwise on the verge of starvation in a refugee center in El Salvador),[5] keeping them alive for a week should be considered a substantial accomplishment, even if they eventually perish because enough others did not join in the relief effort.

Of course, there is a certain simplification in such appeals. Nevertheless, depending on the level of collective activity, it may be reasonable to attribute particular marginal effects to contributions of a given size. At any rate, to resist all such appeals systematically on empirical grounds—claiming that they will never really make a difference—would be to indulge in self-serving cynicism. In the examples discussed here, I will assume that at least *some* charitable appeals for famine relief can be taken at face value.

The perplexity of this argument results because small sacrifices, if large enough in number, add up to heroic totals. And our usual criteria for differentiating obligations and supererogatory acts of heroism are inadequate for this kind of case. Yet, these same criteria are adequate when smaller numbers are involved. A small number of minor sacrifices would not add up to anything significant. And if the sacrifices were more than insignificant to begin with, then a principle of only minimal altruism would not obligate us to make them. It

---

5. "Joint Appeal for Central American Refugees," in the *New York Times*, Jan. 25, 1981, p. 22E.

is only when the numbers are large enough that a principle as weak as merely minimal altruism can entail requirements for sacrifice so great that they add up to heroic proportions.

Here we have two criteria: First, the principle of (at least) minimal altruism (if we can save a human life at minor sacrifice, we are obligated to do so) and second, the cutoff for heroism, which specifies some limit on the sacrifice that can be demanded as a matter of obligation (some sacrifices are *beyond* the call of duty). These two criteria coexist perfectly well at the small scale. But when the number of acts falling under the first principle becomes large enough, then those acts also fall under the second. The coexistence of the two criteria breaks down at the large scale, for we end up classifying the same acts as both obligatory, on the one hand, and beyond the call of duty, on the other.

I do not have an easy answer to this problem of our obligations to contribute to famine relief. My aim, rather, is to offer a diagnosis for why choices such as this are not only emotionally agonizing but also theoretically perplexing. They require that we rethink, in a radical way, the obligations of individuals for the solution of large-scale problems.

The cutoff for heroism—the notion that there are limits on what any other person can demand of us as a matter of duty or obligation—underlies the way most of us think about morality and the way most of us live. Perhaps it is incorrect; but to give it up would represent a great change in our common moral life. In the next sections, I shall introduce certain other assumptions which, I believe, perform the same role. Together these assumptions comprise what I shall call the *basic structure of individual morality*. The central thesis of this book is that, at the large scale, this basic structure is incompatible with the admission of one other assumption which most of us find deeply appealing—namely, that we have at least some positive *general obligations*. By a general obligation, I mean one that is not special or limited to certain particular others by previous agreement, consent, or kinship. A general obligation is one that anyone has, in the appropriate circumstances, to any other person. It is the notion, in other words, that there are at least some things that any other human being owes us (or that we owe them) if we each find ouselves in the appropriate circumstances. By a positive obligation, I mean an obligation not merely to refrain from acting but to perform certain acts. There are many complexities about this notion of positive general obligations. which we shall explore in section 5. For the moment, however, this brief characterization should suffice.

My argument is that at the large scale we cannot admit both (a) the basic structure of individual morality, and (b) the notion of positive general obligations. Either b or some element of a must be given up or reformulated. In part III, I will explore the possible responses to this dilemma. My point will be that every possible way out would represent a very great revision in the way we commonly think and act.

What do I mean by the "large scale"? This book will investigate the moral implications of increasing numbers in three related senses:

1. the number of obligation-determining *situations*,
2. the number of *recipients* or persons who could be affected by actions of a given kind,
3. the number of *actors* or persons who could perform actions of a given kind.

Depending upon the precise formulation of a principle of general obligation, breakdowns in the basic structure of individual morality may result from increases in numbers along any of these three dimensions. My general argument in part I is that certain patterns of breakdown are inevitable—for any possible principle of general obligation.[6]

---

6. Here, as elsewhere, I will sometimes refer to positive general obligations simply as "general obligations." However, I will, unless expressly noted, mean to refer to principles that conform to both requirements. See section 5.

Furthermore, this vulnerability is not merely a theoretical curiosity. In part II, I will argue that principles of general obligation which we commonly accept break down for large-scale cases that *routinely* arise in contemporary life. These perplexities are not only theoretically unavoidable for possible cases, but they are also practically unavoidable for real cases that face most of us if we only bother to think about them.

This argument has a further implication for political theory. The assumptions that produce this breakdown have broad appeal, but they have a special importance for liberalism. It is characteristically liberal assumptions that require us, too easily, as individuals to assume the full burdens of large-scale public problems—those that might better be left to collectivities, nation-states, and other large institutions. We must rethink, in other words, the limits of individual responsibility for problems that should more appropriately be placed in the sphere of *social* choice.

If I may hazard a comparison to democratic theory: until about the end of the eighteenth century, the notion of democracy was thought to be simply inapplicable to the large-scale nation-state. It had to be dramatically reformulated, via the crucial innovation of the concept of representation, in order to be applied at the large scale.[7] My basic claim in this essay is that the ethics of individual responsibility and obligation must also be reformulated if it is to be properly applicable when large enough numbers are involved. Some analogous innovation is required. Although I have no precise blueprint for the shape that innovation should take, I intend to explore systematically here the problems we face without it.

---

7. Robert A. Dahl and Edward R. Tufte, *Size and Democracy* (Stanford, Calif.: Stanford University Press, 1973), pp. 4–12.

2. Three Kinds of Acts

In this essay, I will assume a three-part division in individual morality.[1] First, some actions involve no moral questions at all. They fall within a sphere of permissibly free personal choice. Actions of this kind involve no moral "oughts." They are neither right, nor wrong, good nor bad. This is the sphere of action where, morally speaking, we can do as we please. I will refer to it here as the *zone of moral indifference*.

Second, other actions are classified as right or wrong, good or bad. These are actions that we are required, obligated, or duty-bound to perform (if they are right or good) or not to perform (if they are wrong or bad). It is not only the case that we are right or morally admirable to conform to these pre-scriptions; we would also be wrong or morally blameworthy not to. We are morally blameworthy if we fail to do the right thing or if we do the wrong thing. I will refer to this sphere of action as the *zone of moral requirement*. This is a deliberate simplification of terminology. Within this general category, I will include together kinds of actions that are often distin-

---

1. Both Urmson and Feinberg convincingly criticize another, simpler trichotomous scheme of classification that has undeserved currency: (a) duties or obligations, (b) permissible actions, and (c) prohibited actions. This simpler classification leaves out supererogation and is vulnerable on other grounds. The differences between this scheme and the one employed here should be obvious. See J. O. Urmson, "Saints and Heroes," in Joel Feinberg, ed., *Moral Concepts* (Oxford: Oxford University Press, 1969), pp. 60–73; and Joel Feinberg, "Supererogation and Rules," in *Doing and Deserving: Essays in the Theory of Responsibility* (Princeton: Princeton University Press, 1970), pp. 3–24.

guished: duties and obligations, right actions and good ones, bad actions and wrong ones (when these notions are used to imply requirement rather than supererogation, see below). Some moral positions emphasize these distinctions; others do not. Because the argument offered here is meant to apply *generally* to a wide variety of moral positions, we will have no need to introduce such subdivisions into the zone of moral requirement. This is not to deny that these distinctions are useful for certain purposes; they are not, however, necessary for ours.[2]

Third, some actions fit neither of these two classifications. These actions fall under a different sense of "ought" from that employed above, one which conveys the notion that there are things we "ought" to do but which we would not be morally blameworthy or wrong for failing to do. In this discretionary sense of "ought" it would be admirable or virtuous if we were to do what we "ought," but no one could reasonably blame us if we did not. This classification is normally applied to heroic actions, saintly actions, and those "beyond the call of duty." This is the zone of supererogation. [3]

A deep perplexity results if an action falls into more than one of these categories. Such occasions yield classifications that are not only logically untenable but also morally troubling. For they lead us to inconsistent results about what we ought to do—or whether, in a moral sense, we ought to do anything at all.

Let us distinguish a weak and a strong sense of "ought." If

---

2. Even those who sharply distinguish duties and obligations often admit that, as John Simmons notes, "there is no denying the strong tendency in ordinary language to use these two terms interchangeably." John Simmons, *Moral Principles and Political Obligations* (Princeton: Princeton University Press, 1979), p. 11. For more on the distinction between duties and obligation, see Richard Brandt, "The Concepts of Obligation and Duty," *Mind* 73 (1964); 374–93; E. J. Lemmon, "Moral Dilemmas," *The Philosophical Review* 71 (1962); 139–58; and Joel Feinberg, "Duties, Rights and Claims," in his *Rights, Justice and the Bounds of Liberty: Essays in Social Philosophy* (Princeton: Princeton University Press, 1980), pp. 130–42.

I ought to do X in the weak sense, it would be admirable or morally praiseworthy of me to do so. This weak sense of ought does not, however, include the additional claim that if I fail to conform to such an "ought" I am morally blameworthy for that failure. Moral judgments restricted to this weak sense of ought fall into the zone of supererogation.

By the strong sense of ought, I mean the ought of moral requirement. It is not only morally praiseworthy that we fulfill our duties and obligations, it is also morally *required* that we do so. We are blameworthy if we fail to do so. It is not only right to fulfill obligations, it is also wrong not to. Hence, the strong sense of ought includes the claim of the weak sense that it would be good or morally admirable if we performed a given action; in addition the strong sense adds the proviso that failing to conform to the requirement would be blameworthy or wrong.

With these basic distinctions in mind, we can picture this general threefold division in the table below. (I have changed the order so as to exhibit these relations more clearly.)

	Indifferent Acts	Supererogatory Acts	Required Acts
Strong "ought"	-	-	+
Weak "ought"	-	+	+

If an action falls under neither the strong nor the weak sense of ought, then it must be morally indifferent. If it falls under the weak sense of ought alone, then it is supererogatory. If it falls under both senses of ought, then it is required. Because the strong sense of ought is defined here as implying the weak sense, these are the only logically consistent possibilities (we could not, in other words, have a denial of the weak sense and an assertion of the strong sense as a viable category).

I will assume throughout this essay that actions must be classifiable under no more than one of these three categories.

Of course, there may be cases where we are unsure what moral conclusions to draw about a given action. But no satisfactory classification of an action can place it at *more* than one of these positions. If we have arrived at such a multiple classification, then something has gone awry. Such a multiple classification must be untenable, both logically and morally, for it entails incompatible claims about whether there is something that we are required to do or that we "ought" to do. Let us call this premise the unique classification assumption, as follows:

> THE UNIQUE CLASSIFICATION ASSUMPTION: *A given action must be classifiable at no more than one of the following categories: (a) indifference, (b) moral requirement, (c) supererogation.*[3]

In part II, I will argue that a variety of plausible principles which conform to this unique classification assumption at the small scale, nevertheless yield such multiple classifications at the large scale under realistic assumptions. In the meantime, let us turn to other elements of the basic structure that share this vulnerability to breakdown.

---

3. This three-part classification is worth comparing to a five-part division proposed by David A. J. Richards, *A Theory of Reasons for Action* (Oxford: Oxford University Press, 1971), p. 106:

> (i) right acts which are in accord with moral duties and obligations, and thus which one has no moral right not to do; (ii) wrong acts which omit to do what moral duties and obligations require, and thus which one has no moral right to do; (iii) right acts which are morally at liberty, and which are morally indifferent, e.g. acts pursuing prudential rationality within the constraints of right; (iv) right acts which are in accord with the principles of supererogation, and which it is good to do, but which we are morally at liberty to do, and thus have a right to do or not to do; and (v) wrong acts which omit to do what principles of supererogation require, and which it is bad and offensive to do, and thus have a right to do or not to do.

Richards's categories *i* and *ii* fall into our sphere of requirement; Richards's category *iii* is our sphere of indifference; Richards's categories *iv* and *v* fall into our sphere of supererogation.

3. Sacrifice and Heroism

We have already mentioned the second element of the basic structure of individual morality, which I believe should prove no more controversial than the first. It is that there are limits to the sacrifice which can be demanded of any individual as a matter of duty or obligation. Beyond those limits, an action is heroic. And there is a presumption that such heroic actions must be supererogatory.

This assumption about sacrifice applies only to actions that would otherwise be required or obligatory. Consider Feinberg's example of "the dedicated crackpot who nearly freezes to death trying to convert the indifferent Eskimos to Caribbean voodooism."[1] If we do not believe the action would be required if it involved less sacrifice, we cannot consider it beyond the call of duty merely because the sacrifice is increased. Let us define the general notion:

CUTOFF FOR HEROISM: *Certain levels of sacrifice cannot be morally required of any given individual.*

There are limits, in other words, on what can be demanded of someone as a matter of obligation. Beyond those limits, an act is "beyond the call of duty." And the presumption is that such heroic behavior must be classified as supererogatory, not obligatory.

By "sacrifice" in this definition I mean a reversal or harm

---

1. Joel Feinberg, *Doing and Deserving*, p. 12.

to an agent's interests. I mean to include cases not only of actual sacrifice but also of sufficiently serious *risks* of sacrifice. If Jones jumps into a burning building at great risk to himself in order to save a life, we might consider the act beyond the call of duty if it should turn out that he emerges without a scratch. He knowingly placed himself at risk to a greater degree than could reasonably have been *demanded* of him as a matter of duty or obligation.

Of course, there are difficulties in the definition of appropriate "levels" of sacrifice. Different theories will assess interests in different ways. Some will focus on an agent's actual conception of his own interest. Others will focus on certain criteria for interests that apply regardless of an agent's own actual preferences in the matter. Rawls's theory of primary goods offers one example of the latter kind of theory whereas utilitarianism offers an example of the former.[2] I do not need to settle this question here. The reader may fill in his own favorite theory for assessing the interests sacrificed by an agent. The examples we shall employ should count as severe sacrifices by virtually any plausible criterion.

It should be noted that any such complete version of a theory will have to include some method for discounting sacrifices over time. A dime donated each month for ten years will not represent the same sacrifice, or the same investment, as twelve dollars donated at one time. Since different theories for assessing interests may differ crucially in their treatment of time, I will confine my application of the cutoff to sacrifices that are concentrated within a relatively brief period so that such temporal questions should not add controversy to the claim that those cases amount to severe sacrifices.

One strategy for developing this argument would have tied it to a particular theory of extreme sacrifice. I have, in fact, invested considerable effort in one such theory, presented

2. For a general discussion of the problem of assessing interests, see my *Tyranny and Legitimacy: A Critique of Political Theories* (Baltimore: Johns Hopkins, 1979), chapter 3.

elsewhere.[3] However, the argument of this book is, I believe, general in its application to a wide range of moral positions. There is no reason to rest it on one particular substantive criterion for assessing interests. The general argument of section 7 should apply to *any* such theory of interests. Furthermore, the particular examples employed to illustrate the argument should be fairly noncontroversial, regardless of particular substantive conceptions.

In order to preserve the general application of the argument, I shall not propose any particular cutoff for levels of sacrifice in the above definition. My argument will only require the assumption that there is *some* limit. Proponents of different moral positions may reasonably disagree about any particular demarcation. I mean for my argument to apply to all of these positions. In this sense, each reader may fill in his own notions about the appropriate limits. Our basic theoretical results will not be altered—although unusually high or low limits may affect some particular examples.

It is also worth noting that the limits may change for different kinds of acts and for different kinds of obligations. It may be possible to demand greater sacrifice from special obligations to which one has consented than from general obligations. So long as there is *some* limit corresponding to any given kind of act and to any given kind of obligation, the assumption holds. No matter what the principle of obligation, if the sacrifice is great enough, it should be viewed at some point as "beyond the call of duty."

Another point worth noting about this definition is that it does not distinguish the sacrifice of an individual act from the sacrifice produced by numerous acts. Consider a relief worker during an epidemic. Perhaps his chance of catching the dread disease from contact with any given victim is small. Yet, we might imagine that if he comes into contact with a large enough number, the cumulative risk is so great that we might

---

3. Ibid., part I.

classify his overall conduct as *beyond* the call of duty. Even though the marginal risk of each act of assistance is small, the total adds up to heroic proportions.[4] Because it is experienced over the life history of the same individual, it seems appropriate to include the total risk or sacrifice in assessing the conduct of that individual. If the cutoff were applied only to acts considered in isolation from all other acts, then individuals could be vulnerable to enormous total costs without any recognition that their sacrifice from many acts amounted, in total, to heroic proportions. It would seem morally arbitrary to apply the cutoff for heroism to a single act but not to numerous acts by the same agent when the sacrifice incurred amounts to the same.

That there are limits to the sacrifice which can be demanded as a matter of obligation is a commonplace assumption in recent moral theory. This assumption can be found in David Richards's ambitious attempt to construct moral principles for individuals from Rawls's theory of social justice.[5] It can also be found among utilitarians. J. O. Urmson, for example, in his well-known article "Saints and Heroes," concludes that "utilitarianism can best accommodate the facts to which I have drawn attention," namely, in the case of acts of heroism, that some acts are "beyond the call of duty" because of the sacrifices they involve.[6] Following Mill's distinction between acts that can be exacted from a man like a debt (obligations), and those that have moral value but "whose omission cannot be called wrong-doing" (acts of supererogation), Urmson

---

4. I adapt this example from Urmson, "Saints and Heroes," and from Feinberg, "Supererogation and Rules." For my purposes, I need not enter into the question of how much sacrifice should trigger the cutoff. Note Feinberg's proposal: "the sacrifice *normally* involved in doing of a duty" (emphasis in original), ibid., p. 11. For a discussion of how sufficient self-sacrifice is almost universally identified with heroism, see William J. Goode, *The Celebration of Heroes: Prestige as a Control System* (Berkeley: University of California Press, 1978), pp. 343–45.

5. David A. J. Richards, *A Theory of Reasons for Action*, pp. 95–96.

6. Urmson, "Saints and Heroes," p. 72.

poses a classic case of heroism—a soldier who "sacrifices his life by throwing himself on the grenade and protecting his comrades with his own body." Such an act of heroism cannot be considered obligatory:

> ...if the soldier had not thrown himself on the grenade would he have failed in his duty? Though clearly, he is superior in some way to his comrade, can we possibly say that they failed in their duty by not trying to be the one who sacrificed himself? If he had not done so, could anyone have said to him, "You ought to have thrown yourself on that grenade"? Could a superior have decently ordered him to do it? The answer to all of these questions is plainly negative.[7]

Writing from a perspective different from both of these, Judith Thomson offers a distinction that makes fundamentally the same point—the distinction between "Good Samaritans" and "Minimally Decent Samaritans." Although we are not morally obligated to undertake sacrifices so great as those involved in being "Good Samaritans," she argues, we are required to be "minimally decent." Thomson brings up the famous case of Kitty Genovese, whose brutal and laborious murder was witnessed by thirty-eight people in adjacent apartments, who did nothing to help her—even though they could have called the police without risk to themselves. Thomson argues that "Good Samaritans would have rushed out to give direct assistance against the murderer." But this is too much to *require* morally because it would involve too great a risk. Her objection to the thirty-eight witnesses, however, is not that they failed to be heroic in this way. It is that "they did not even trouble to pick up a phone to call the police. Minimally Decent Samaritanism

---

7. Ibid., p. 63.

would call for their doing at least that, and their not having done it was monstrous."[8]

Although they are not obligated to save a life if the risk is sufficiently great, if the risk is small enough they are morally required to do so.

8. Judith Jarvis Thomson, "A Defense of Abortion," in Marshall Cohen, Thomas Nagel, and Thomas Scanlon eds., The Rights and Wrongs of Abortion (Princeton: Princeton University Press, 1974), pp. 3–22. The quotation is from page 19.

4. The Zone of Indifference

An unspoken assumption of our everyday lives is that morality is reserved for special occasions. Most of the actions that we perform are neither right nor wrong, good nor bad. They fall, rather, within the zone of moral indifference. Within the way of life that most of us take for granted, the occasions upon which our actions are morally determined for us—or present us with explicitly moral conflicts—are relatively rare.

If this were not the case, then we could not be free in a sense that we habitually assume,[1] for there would be no significant sphere of action where we could feel at liberty to do as

---

1. See Isaiah Berlin, "Two Concepts of Liberty," in Isaiah Berlin, *Four Essays on Liberty* (Oxford: Oxford University Press, 1969), pp. 118–72. I believe this connection between negative liberty and the zone of indifference is implicit in Berlin's discussion in that he treats conformity with the moral law (the Kantian notion of autonomy) as a species of positive, not negative, freedom. The sphere of negative freedom is the area of life within which we are free from the coercive restraints of moral, legal, and social requirements (the tyranny of opinion). It is the sphere of permissibly free personal choice. This point is more explicit in Hart, who discusses all obligations (moral as well as legal) as "interferences with freedom." See H. L. A. Hart, "Are There Any Natural Rights?" in Anthony Quinton, ed., *Political Philosophy* (Oxford: Oxford University Press, 1967), pp. 53–66. This point is also compatible with MacCallum's critique of Berlin and his alternative formulation: "Taking the format X is (is not) free from y to do (not do, become, not become) Z; Z ranges over agents, y ranges over such 'preventing conditions' as constraints, restrictions, interferences and barriers, and Z ranges over actions or conditions of character or circumstances." Gerald C. MacCallum, Jr., "Negative and Positive Freedom," in Peter Laslett, W. G. Runciman, and Quentin Skinner, eds., *Philosophy, Politics and Society*, Fourth Series (Oxford: Basil Blackwell, 1972), pp. 174–93; the quotation is from p. 176.

we please. Our moral notions—when applied to our particular circumstances—would always obligate us to do some things rather than others—or they would confront us with cases of conflicting moral claims and, hence, problems of conscious moral decision.[2] Yet, in the way most of us live, morality does not intrude so pervasively. Rather, it presents itself only on occasions that are especially serious—or even momentous.

To take some present examples from my own life, is it a *moral* question what my wife and I serve at a dinner party? Or what courses I decide to teach next fall? Is it a moral question what law school my brother decides to attend? Or even, to take a question of greater importance, is it a *moral* problem that my wife and I should consider when we discuss whether or not—or when—to have a second child?

Under some possible conditions any of these questions might pose a moral problem. But under normal conditions most of us would not think about them in that way. The way of life we assume would permit us, as a matter of course, to classify these actions, and a host of others, within the zone of moral indifference—the realm of permissibly free personal choice.[3]

If I am incorrect in this assumption, then two results would immediately follow. The most obvious result would be that most of us must be immoral in the entire way of life we take for granted. For we would then be ignoring a host of obligations as a matter of course. Unless by blind luck we always do the right thing anyway—without even being aware

---

2. I include ties within the case of conflicting moral claims. So it may be precisely, equally good (or required) for A to do X or Y. While A may then, in the economist's sense, be "indifferent" between X and Y (if his preferences conform to the stated moral position) both X and Y are placed within the zone of moral requirement as compared to other actions which raise no moral issues and fall within what I have called the zone of indifference.

3. See Fried's discussion of the "discretionary domain" for a similar view on this issue. Charles Fried, *Right and Wrong* (Cambridge, Mass.: Harvard University Press, 1978), chapter 1, plus pp. 167–68, 171–72, 183–85, 194.

of the moral questions involved—we must be subject to a host of failed obligations of both omission and commission.

The second result of sacrificing the zone of indifference would be that we would all be obligated to be "saints." We would have to begin living in such a way that virtually every action or inaction we considered—at every moment in our lives—would be treated as a problem of moral choice. Of course, in order to simplify deliberation we might arrive at certain general rules of thumb for particular kinds of cases. But we would, nevertheless, have to regard the actions falling under those rules of thumb as morally required.

If we succeeded in regulating all of our actions in this way, then our entire way of life would become "a case of duty done by virtue of self-control in a context in which most men would be led astray by inclination or self-interest."[4] Urmson plausibly defines "saintly" behavior in this way; his point, however, is to claim that such behavior is not required but supererogatory. Yet, the result of sacrificing the zone of indifference would be that we would all be required to be saints. This is as troubling, I believe, as the case mentioned earlier in which we were, apparently, obligated to be heroic.

I will assume here that saintly behavior, however admirable, is not morally required of us all. In other words, my working assumption throughout this essay will be that the way of life most of us have adopted is not, on its face, immoral. It is neither hypocrisy nor wickedness that permits us to insulate much of our lives from the conscious intrusion of moral requirements. This insulation is, in fact, a presupposition of a kind of negative freedom that most of us take for granted—the freedom, within outer limits set by morality, to do as we please in broad areas of our lives.

I will assume, in other words, that under normal conditions we are justified in regarding the zone of moral indifference as applying to a robust proportion of our actions. I may,

---

4. Urmson, "Saints and Heroes," p. 61.

of course, be mistaken in this assumption. Some venerable views have, indeed, supported a quite different conclusion.[5] But most readers are probably willing to entertain the hypothesis that I am not mistaken in this assumption—for the morality of their entire way of life depends upon it. Let us define this assumption more precisely as follows:

> THE ROBUST ZONE OF INDIFFERENCE: *A substantial proportion of any individual's actions falls appropriately within the zone of indifference or permissibly free personal choice.*

As in the cutoff for heroism, there is, admittedly, a difficulty in setting particular quantitative standards. I do not need to specify the meaning of "substantial" for the proportion of acts in this definition, just as I did not need to specify the precise amount of sacrifice that renders an act "beyond" the call of duty. For I only need to assume the applicability of some standard. So long as there is some point beyond which any given proponent of a moral position would agree that his zone of indifference no longer applies to a "substantial" proportion of his acts, my argument will apply. There is certainly room for reasonable disagreement on drawing such lines. My argument is meant to apply, however, in a general way across all such disagreements to any position that can be reasonably said to be committed to the three assumptions just

---

5. Plato's ideal of the just man requires such a complete harmony of parts that conforming to it would lead to prescriptions for every aspect of life. See the *Republic*, especially 4.441c–445b. In the F. M. Cornford translation (Oxford: Oxford University Press, 1945), pp. 139–43. Another dissent from this view, on quite different grounds, can be found in G. E. Moore: "Our 'duty,' therefore can only be defined as that action, which will cause more good to exist in the universe than any other possible alternative. And what is 'right' or 'morally permissible' only differs from this, as what will *not* cause less good than any possible alternative." Moore, *Principia Ethica* (Cambridge: Cambridge University Press, 1903; reprinted, 1966), p. 148. This variant of what we will later call "strict consequentialism" obviously leaves no room for a robust sphere of indifference.

defined: the unique classification assumption, the cutoff for heroism, and the robust zone of indifference.

These assumptions are meant to apply to ordinary citizens under normal conditions that still need to be specified. For we can imagine public officials and other persons subject to unusually demanding special obligations for whom these assumptions—particularly the robust sphere of indifference—may not be appropriate. Let us turn now to the distinction between *special* and *general* obligations and then, in section 6, we will specify the normal conditions under which this argument is meant to apply.

5. General Obligations

Some obligations are based on a special history of relations among the parties or a particular role voluntarily accepted by at least one of the parties. I have obligations to my mother that I do not have to a total stranger. I also have obligations to my students and to my colleagues. Similarly, I may have obligations to particular persons based on consent, promises, or contracts. To use the terminology made familiar by Hart, these are *special obligations* that are limited to the parties involved.[1]

But are there at least some obligations that I may have to another person apart from any special history of relations between us and apart from any previous acts of consent, promises, or other agreements? The issue is admittedly controversial, but from an impartial moral perspective—one from which I view myself as just one person among others— such special relations as those just mentioned would not appear to be the decisive consideration in determining all my obligations. From such an impartial perspective, it would be difficult to avoid admitting some duties or obligations that *any* of us could owe to *anyone* else, including a total stranger.

Principles of general obligation raise many complex issues. Although no attempt to deal with all of them is likely to

---

1. "Are There Any Natural Rights?" See also William N. Nelson, "Special Rights, General Rights and Social Justice," *Philosophy and Public Affairs* 3 (1974): 410–30, and Simmons, *Moral Principles and Political Obligations,* chapters 1 and 2.

prove entirely satisfactory, I hope to arrive at a serviceable account here. By "serviceable" I mean an account that will permit us to complete our general argument and that plausibly applies to the more obvious particular cases of principles we would wish to include in this category. I will not, however, presume to dispatch every disputed boundary issue. There is likely to remain some controversy about whether or not any particular formulation falls into the category of principles of general obligation.

First, I will assume that principles of general obligation are *principles* rather than merely particular judgments. They are formulated so as to apply to all possible relevantly similar cases. Because they are *universal*, they apply to an open-ended class of possible events. We cannot enumerate all of the possible instances to which the principle may apply. If we could, it would be, not a principle, but rather a particular judgment designed to apply only to a singular event (or a finite list of singular events). "J. F. ought to do A rather than B on September 30, 1980" applies only to such a singular event. Perhaps Hare is right that by the meaning of "ought" such a particular judgment commits us implicitly to some universal principle. But such a universal principle would require some specification of relevant similarity for other possible cases. A moral principle, as opposed to a particular judgment, must be formulated so that its criteria for applying to relevantly similar cases are spelled out.[2]

This universal character of moral principles will play a role in our argument below. For if a moral principle is universal, then it must always be possible to imagine more cases falling under it. As relevantly similar cases increase in number, the obligations for *anyone* entailed by a principle of general obligation increase so as to overload the basic structure of individual morality. Because a principle of general

---

2. See R. M. Hare, *Freedom and Reason* (Oxford: Oxford University Press, 1963), particularly chapter 3, "Principles."

obligation must be universal in form, we know that it must, in theory, be applicable to such increasing numbers of relevantly similar cases.

Now, of course, this property of moral principles applies as well to principles of special obligation. The crucial difference is that as more relevantly similar cases fall under a principle of *special* obligation, they do not necessarily determine further obligations for *me* (or for any other given person). Those cases determine obligations only for those who have consented, promised or come to occupy the relevant roles. Furthermore, we can all limit, if we choose, our liability to increases in special obligations by not consenting or promising or occupying the relevant roles. As we shall see, we cannot limit our liability to general obligations in this way.

Such a general obligation is one that is owed *by* anyone *to* anyone. Let us explore this notion more carefully. I will assume that any principle of obligation must specify a *description of obligation-determining situations*, i.e., situations in which those obligations obtain. If such a description corresponds to a *general* obligation, then it must satisfy a kind of *anonymity* condition explained as follows:

> GENERAL OBLIGATIONS: *An obligation is* general *if it would be unaffected by exchanging the identity of the agent and the identity of the recipients with those of any other persons (who could satisfy the required descriptions).*

By the "agent" I mean the person who is to perform the action. By the "recipients" I mean any other persons who appear in the description of the obligation-determining situation (typically, any persons affected by the action).[3] Now,

---

3. This definition can be interpreted to permit other moral actors to be regarded, in a sense, as recipients for some kinds of moral principles ("interdependent" ones in the sense defined in section 8). Although this usage may seem odd at first, note that if I am one of the others who is morally required to do an action of a given kind, I am, in a recognizable sense, affected

certain kinds of rigged definite descriptions could be devised that would trivialize this anonymity requirement. For this reason, certain limitations must be placed on *admissible descriptions* for general obligations in the above definition. For there are many particularizing characteristics of individuals that would render an obligation *special* rather than *general* if those characteristics were built into the definition. Descriptions specifying persons with particular names or identities, occupants of particular roles, persons with special abilities or competence, membership in certain groups (e.g., racial, sexual, religious, ethnic), or a history of having committed previous acts—particularly, past agreements, promises, or acts of consent would all have this result.[4] I will interpret the anonymity requirement broadly so that *none* of these particularizing characteristics may be specified in the definition of the agent or the recipients in a principle of general obligation. These are all characteristics that persons may bring *with* them to the exchange specified above; they are not, however, requirements of eligibility for being subject to the obligation or for helping to determine someone else's obligations. This limitation on admissible descriptions will prevent the anonymity condition from being trivialized. Otherwise, for example, a principle such as "Everyone should obey J. F." could count as a general obligation principle because another person could trade places with me without altering the

---

by the action. For the particular principles of general obligation examined in part II, the only recipients discussed will be those who are affected by an action (either in a causal sense or in the moral sense that their rights or entitlements are altered). Strictly speaking, other actors mentioned in the generalization argument could, by this definition of recipience, be regarded as *both* agents and recipients. This does not affect our argument, but it will simplify the discussion if we consider them under the category of agents rather than recipients in part II.

4. I include within "previous acts" the act of having conformed to a given moral principle in the past. See the discussion of "agent-specific" principles in section 19.

obligations—in the thin sense that if *he* were J. F., he could command everyone's obedience according to this principle.

The impartial moral appeal of general obligations is captured by the notion of anyone changing places with anyone else. Hence, the description should not be encumbered by *particularizing characteristics* that limit either the range of *actors* subject to the obligation or the range of persons who could, at least in theory, find themselves in the position of *recipients* on some possible occasion. For example, "Everyone should obey his (own respective) sister" limits both the range of actors and the range of recipients. "Everyone should obey the police chief of New Haven" does not limit the range of actors. Its admissibility depends on the range of availability of the position of recipient (in this case "police chief of New Haven"). My proposal is that the position of either actor or recipient should be *universally available* in the sense that any person should be able to occupy it without alteration in central elements of the present identity or previous history of that person or anyone else. Hence, reference to pain and suffering on the part of recipients would be admissible, because any person could experience pain and suffering without alteration of his or her present identity or previous history. But, I assume that *any* person could not become police chief of New Haven without alteration of his or her previous history. That is part of the meaning of a special role with special qualifications.

Similarly, I could not become a member of various racial, sexual, religious, or ethnic groups without altering central elements of my present identity and previous history. Hence, such descriptions would rule me out of participation as either actor or recipient in some formulations. Principles requiring such descriptions would thus determine special rather than general obligations. Whereas I could *imagine* myself subject to the exchange of positions, if properly altered to conform to the particularizing characteristics, I could not put myself in the required position with my present identity and previous history.[5] Only if virtually *anyone* could participate in this kind of exchange would the description become admissible for a principle of general obligation.

Or consider "Everyone should obey his or her (own respective) parents." Even granting what may certainly be questioned—that everyone has parents—such a principle would not withstand the *exchange* requirement (specified above) for any particular application of the description to an obligation-determining situation. For even if everyone may have or may, in theory, become a parent, once identities are exchanged with any other person, the obligation in any particular situation no longer holds. I might, in other words be obligated to obey *my* mother (by such a principle), but I am not obligated to obey *yours*.

Consider another possible particularizing characteristic, abilities. If an action is described in such a way that it requires *special abilities or competence,* then I will assume that a description of such abilities or competence falls within the range of particularizing characteristics which delimit special, rather than general, obligations. A doctor may save a life with trivial effort under conditions where the efforts of an ordinary person would be useless. A principle that requires efforts from the doctor but never from the ordinary person will be considered a special obligation principle. A principle, on the other hand, that requires certain efforts from *either* could be considered a general obligation principle.

The intuitive idea is that principles of general obligation

5. See Rawls's requirement that a principle be both "universal" in application and "general" in form (lacking "rigged definite descriptions" of particular persons), *A Theory of Justice* (Cambridge, Mass.: Harvard University Press, 1971), pp. 130–36. See also Mackie's useful distinction between different forms of "universalization," although my proposal is closer to his second than to his third stage. John Mackie, *Ethics: Inventing Right and Wrong* (New York: Penguin, 1977), chapter 4. His third stage, in which I put myself in your shoes with *your* preferences, history, etc., would trivialize our exchange requirement in the manner discussed above.

should determine what can be demanded *of* anyone *by* anyone. The abilities required to meet such demands should be broadly shared, if not universal. The capabilities specified in the description, in other words, should be no more than what could ordinarily be *expected* of anyone—in this sense, they should be *ordinary* capacities rather than *special* ones. In the Kitty Genovese case referred to earlier, a deaf-mute would not be able to telephone the police, but the capacity to do so would be *expected* of any ordinary member of this society. The argument that follows will be taken to apply to all persons who have, at least, ordinary capacities in this sense.

This anonymity requirement is intended to rule out the factors that typically determine *special* as opposed to *general* obligations, e.g., the attainment of special capacities, the previous history of relations among the parties (kinship, consent, promises), or the occupation of some particular role (and, hence, positional duties of a role-related kind).

Principles that satisfy this requirement for general obligations are a familiar part of our common moral conceptions. The principle of minimal altruism mentioned in section 1 is an example. *Anyone* who can save a human life at minor cost is obligated to do so. The identity of the agent is limited only by ability to perform the required act in the appropriate circumstances. Furthermore, the identity of the recipient may be exchanged with that of any other person. It does not matter *whose* life would be saved. Anyone else could trade places with the person in question and the obligation would remain unchanged.

Generalization arguments that would require one to do an action when "everyone doing the same" would produce good consequences (or that would require one to refrain from an action when "everyone doing the same" would produce bad consequences) are similarly general in this sense. I could trade places with anyone else who could do the action and the obligation would remain unchanged; likewise, the persons affected could trade places with others who were similarly affected, and the mere identities of the recipients would not alter the obligations.

The principle of minimal altruism and the generalization argument (in a variety of forms) will concern us in some detail in part II. But the range of general obligation principles is much broader. We might imagine a quite different kind of principle—that "one must act so as to exemplify the ideal of virtue whenever possible." Such a principle conforms equally to the requirements for general obligations. Or, to take a more arbitrary example, "Whenever the sky is cloudy, one must sacrifice a sheep on the altar of the gods." Even though, presumably, none of us would subscribe to such a principle, it illustrates the variety of possible principles of general obligation.

Or consider a principle of altruism more demanding than the merely "minimal" one already mentioned. Rawls includes the "duty of mutual aid" among the "natural duties" that could be derived from the original position. This is "the duty of helping another when he is in need or jeopardy, provided that one can do so without excessive risk or loss to oneself." Here the cases of need are broader than the saving of life mentioned in minimal altruism. Furthermore, the sacrifices demanded are not merely "minor" ones. One can be required to run substantial, but not "excessive," risks or losses. Rawls's natural duties, such as this duty of mutual aid, are "general obligations" in the sense defined here: "they hold between persons irrespective of their institutional relationship; they obtain between all as equal moral persons. In this sense, the natural duties are owed not only to definite individuals, say to those cooperating together in a particular social arrangement, but to persons generally." Unlike special obligations, "they apply to us without regard for our voluntary acts."[6] As one commentator notes: "These duties are

---

6. Rawls, *Theory of Justice*, pp. 114, 115.

owed *by all persons to all others* and form the core of what used to be known as "Natural Law."[7]

General obligations may thus assume a variety of familiar forms. My argument will be that the admission of *any* such principle of general obligation to perform actions on behalf of any other person or group will lead, at the large scale, to the breakdown of the basic structure of individual morality. The reason this is theoretically perplexing is that the basic structure has been defined in a quite minimal way. It consists in no more than the three assumptions already defined—the *unique classification* assumption, the *cutoff for heroism,* and the *robustness of the sphere of indifference.* To give up any of these assumptions, I will argue, would constitute a very great revision in our common moral conceptions. Perhaps such a great revision is necessary. Although such possibilities will be raised in part III, my intention is not to prescribe a way out of this dilemma, but rather to explore its dimensions.

On the other hand, we could maintain the basic structure in its entirety but give up the notion of general obligation. I believe that this is, in its own way, equally troubling. For it would seem a denial of our common humanity not to admit *some* general obligations to perform actions on behalf of any other person, even a total stranger.

Whether we argue from Rawls's "original position,"[8] the "sympathetic spectator" of the classical utilitarians[9] or the Golden Rule,[10] there is a deep appeal in impartial moral perspectives from which we determine our obligations after

---

7. Simmons, *Moral Principles and Political Obligations,* p. 13.

8. Rawls, *Theory of Justice,* pp. 17–22, 118–22.

9. Ibid., pp. 183–92. See also Adam Smith, *The Theory of Moral Sentiments* (Indianapolis: Liberty Classics, 1969), pp. 22, 31, 33, 35, 36, 38, 41, 71, 161–62, 211, 228, 247–49, 352, 371, 422; and Roderick Firth, "Ethical Absolution and the Ideal Observer," *Philosophy and Phenomenological Research* 12 (1952): 317–45.

10. For some recent philosophical discussions of the Golden Rule, see

we have put ourselves in the place of any other person who may be affected by our action or failure to act. This kind of perspective has sometimes been identified with the moral point of view itself. As Thomas Nagel characterizes it:

> I believe that the general form of moral reasoning is to put yourself in other people's shoes. This leads to an impersonal concern for them corresponding to the impersonal concern for yourself. ... In a sense the requirement is that you love your neighbor as yourself; but only as much as you love yourself when you look at yourself from outside with fair detachment.[11]

If we love our neighbors as we love ourselves, we are inexorably led to the admission of at least some positive, general obligations. Of course, the issue turns on how we consider our own interests (how we "love ourselves")—in Nagel's impartial perspective, Rawls's original position, or the impartial spectator model. From any of these perspectives, some principles of general obligation seem undeniable. How would one argue against the principle of minimal altruism, for example, from such a perspective? If I have to consider whether to save a starving refugee at minor cost to myself, after I have put myself realistically in the shoes of the starving refugee, any reasonable calculation of the interests at stake will lead me to conform to the obligation. And the argument is not merely a utilitarian one. From Rawls's original position similar conclusions clearly follow.[12] In any case, from perspectives that many have identified with the general

---

Mackie, Ethics, chapter 4; and Alan Gewirth, Reason and Morality (Chicago: University of Chicago Press, 1978).

11. Thomas Nagel, Mortal Questions (Cambridge: Cambridge University Press, 1979) p. 126.

12. See our discussion in section 19 below and the detailed extensions of the Rawlsian argument in Richards, Theory of Reasons, and for international redistribution, in Charles Beitz, Political Philosophy and International Relations (Princeton: Princeton University Press, 1979), part 3.

form of moral reasoning itself, obligations of this kind are difficult to deny. This is why the second horn of our dilemma—either give up the basic structure or give up such general obligations—is fully as troubling as the first.

At various points I have alluded to a second characteristic of the kind of obligation that leads to the breakdown of the basic structure of individual morality at the large scale. This breakdown arises for obligations that are *both* general and positive. Since positive general obligations will be the only kind explicitly discussed in the arguments that follow, I will sometimes refer to them simply as general obligations. It is, however, important to make the other requirement explicit as well.

The intuitive notion is that positive obligations define moral requirements not merely to refrain or avoid but actually to *perform* certain actions. This familiar idea needs some refinement, however, in its application to omissions. For there are some omissions we might reasonably wish to include within the realm of positive obligations (considering them as actions of a kind) and others that we might not. For example, if, when faced with a range of alternative possible actions that might alter the status quo in various ways, I intentionally do nothing so as to maintain the status quo (or so as to avoid interfering with changes that are already taking place in the status quo), then I have, in a familiar sense, performed a kind of action. To take a crude example, if an animal in my care is starving and I intentionally do not feed it, I have performed a kind of action and can be blamed accordingly—even if my action consists, in a sense, in my having done nothing at all.

This kind of omission might be distinguished from another, looser sense of omission in which it might be said that, in sitting here at my desk writing this essay, I am not going to China, and I am also not violating my neighbor's property rights. Either description of my present action of writing at my desk (as "not going to China" or "not violating my neighbor's property rights"), although true, tells very little about the action that I am, in fact, performing. An obligation to perform an omission of this kind would not, in the context described, count as a positive obligation. In fact, the obligation to avoid interfering with my neighbor's property rights would count as a classic case of a negative (rather than positive) obligation. The general distinction might be formulated as follows:

> POSITIVE OBLIGATIONS: *An agent is under a positive obligation when, from the class of alternative acts available to him (including the act of intentional omission of all the other acts in the class), he can distinguish one or more acts that he is morally required to perform (in preference to all the other alternatives available).*

Hence, a negative requirement such as that one should refrain from violating a neighbor's property rights, will normally be insufficient to determine a positive obligation.[13] For although it rules out certain alternatives, it leaves entirely open the question of how all the rest should be compared. In not violating my neighbor's property rights at time T_1, I might

---

13. A principle of obligation is formulated positively when it *consistently* determines obligations that are "positive" in this sense. However, principles that are clearly *not* positive in this sense may, nevertheless, have positive implications when applied to some special, idiosyncratic circumstances. Suppose I am driving a train and, as I approach a fork in the tracks, I see that if I continue straight ahead I will run into someone. I may be constrained by a characteristically negative prohibition (avoid killing people) to turn at the fork. Notice how the fork in the tracks limits me to only one possible option if I am to avoid imposing certain prohibited effects on someone else. In such a situation, a determinate requirement to *do* something in particular follows from the usually negative prohibition to avoid harm. This example is adapted from one devised by Philippa Foot in "The Problem of Abortion and the Doctrine of Double Effect," in James Rachels, ed., *Moral Problems* (New York: Harper and Row, 1971), pp. 28–41. But because such a prohibition does not consistently determine positive obligations (in fact, it does so only for such extraordinary cases), it would not yield a principle we would classify as positive here. Such a principle must consistently determine positive obligations.

write this essay, I might give to famine relief, I might cast my vote in the presidential election, or I might take my son to nursery school. I am only under a positive obligation if I can distinguish one or more of these possibilities as morally required in preference to the alternatives. If only one is required, then I have no further problem of ethical deliberation. If more than one is required, then I may face a problem of conflicting obligations or duties.[14]

Of course, moral positions will vary according to how they determine the class of acts "available" to an agent at a given time. Some positions will differentiate acts by the different *states of affairs* that are causally connected to performance of those acts. Other positions will differentiate acts by the *intentions* of the agent in performing each possible alternative. Some positions will include (and hold the agent responsible for) alternatives of which the agent is not even aware, but of which he *should* have been aware, had he not been negligent in assessing his obligations.[15] I will not take a particular position on these substantive issues here because my argument is a general one; it is meant to apply to moral positions emphasizing any of these distinctions.

Regardless of the precise criteria for differentiating alternatives, I assume that any adequate moral position committed to a principle of general obligation will offer some basis for determining a class of mutually exclusive alternative acts

---

14. I face either a problem of conflicting obligations (including the case of ties) or a problem of alternative routes to the fulfillment of the same obligation. In either case, a subclass of required alternatives is distinguished from the rest.

15. See G. E. M. Anscombe's discussion of "voluntary ignorance": "when it was necessary and possible for the pilot to navigate and for the cook to put salt in the potatoes, the loss of the ship and the spoiling of the potatoes are ascribed to the pilot and cook as causes....So when it was necessary and possible for A to know, the ignorance is ascribed to A's will as cause." Anscombe, "The Two Kinds of Error in Action," in Judith J. Thomson and Gerald Dworkin, eds., *Ethics* (New York:Harper and Row, 1968), pp. 279–88; the quotation is from page 287.

available to an agent at any given time. Once such a class of alternatives is determined in a particular context, it should be easy to differentiate positive obligations from merely negative ones. Negative obligations merely rule out certain possibilities but are insufficient to select any acts as morally required from the list of mutually exclusive alternatives. An agent is under a positive obligation, on the other hand, when one or more of the alternatives can be specified as morally required. If more than one is required, then he must be faced with a problem of conflicting obligations or duties (or a choice among alternative routes to satisfying the same obligation).[16] And if the act of "doing nothing" so as to omit performance of all the other acts (in the list of mutually exclusive alternatives) is selected, that is itself a specific act falling under a sufficiently determinate description as to constitute a positive obligation in the sense defined here. For if such an act is morally required, one's actions are as clearly determined by principle as they would be if any of the other actions were required instead.

---

16. I assume, however, that each new obligation-determining situation that confronts an agent creates a new obligation and not merely a new alternative route to the satisfaction of a previously existing obligation. Hence, I mention this possibility of alternative routes to satisfying the same obligation for the sake of completeness. It does not play a role in the argument that follows, especially in the general argument of section 7.

6. Other Presuppositions

Some principles specify obligations in such a weak form that they can evade our argument. Prima facie principles, on some interpretations, offer this possibility. If a moral requirement *disappears* whenever it conflicts with any other relevant moral consideration, then its formulation is too weak for our purposes. But prima facie principles in such a weak sense do not appear to do justice to the facts of moral conflict. The true difficulty offered by any of the familiar cases of conflicting obligations is not captured by the notion that one of the alternatives must be *really* right and the other apparent obligation is only illusory. Consider Sartre's famous problem faced by one of his students who had to decide whether to stay with his old and dependent mother or fight in the French Resistance.[1] Or consider Agamemnon's incompatible duties to his fleet and to his daughter. In these cases when one decides that one of the alternatives is, on balance, better, the other remains as an obligation violated. One must experience regret, and, if possible, make reparations or amends.[2]

On some interpretations of prima facie obligations, how-

---

1. Jean-Paul Sartre, "Existentialism Is a Humanism," in Walter Kaufmann, ed., *Existentialism from Dostoevsky to Sartre* (New York: Meridian Books, 1964), pp. 287–311; the example cited is on page 295. It is also discussed by Alasdair MacIntyre in "What Morality Is Not," in G. Wallace and A. D. M. Walker, *The Definition of Morality* (London: Metheun, 1970), pp. 26–39.

2. For a similar view of conflicting obligations, see Bernard Williams's essay, "Ethical Consistency," in his *Problems of the Self* (Cambridge: Cambridge University Press, 1973), pp. 166–86 and, in particular, pp. 172–73.

ever, the obligation that is not honored simply disappears. David Lyons, for example, offers the following model for the role of a ceteris paribus or "other things being equal" clause in a "weak" or prima facie obligation:

If p and q, then r.

where q is the ceteris paribus clause, and p refers to all the other antecedent conditions for a moral requirement r.[3] On this analysis, no requirement for action follows when p is satisfied but q is not, i.e., when "other things" are not equal. The apparent moral requirement then seems to disappear for cases of conflict. Without q being satisfied, no moral conclusions about the action in question follow.

As Lyons implies, some proponents of prima facie principles will be unhappy with this result.[4] In fact, W. D. Ross, who first formulated the notion of prima facie principles, wished to deny this implication. According to Ross, prima facie obligations that are overridden do not disappear. As he puts it, "they are not illusions which we dispense with." For example: "It remains hard fact that an act of promise-breaking is morally unsuitable, even when we decide that in spite of this, it is the act that we ought to do."[5]

For Ross, our "responsibility" does not vanish for failing to conform to the obligation (for example, to keep promises), which is not fulfilled in a case of conflicting obligations. Yet such "responsibility" does not mean that, on balance, we should have done anything different.[6] It may be useful, here, to distinguish: (a) the mere fact that an act is classified within the zone of moral requirement (i.e., that it ought to be done, or

---

3. David Lyons, Forms and Limits of Utilitarianism (Oxford: Oxford University Press, 1965), p. 20.

4. "I am not sure that theorists who employ concepts like 'prima facie right' and 'good reason' will find this result attractive" (ibid., p. 21).

5. Sir W. David Ross, Foundations of Ethics (Oxford: Oxford University Press, 1939), p. 85.

6. Ibid.

that it ought not to be done), and (b) the stronger claim not only that it falls under such a moral requirement but that also, on balance, the moral requirement outweighs any other conflicting moral requirement. An obligation may be *more* than prima facie (at least in Lyons's sense) in that it satisfies *a* but also *less* than a strong or absolute principle of the kind that always satisfies *b*.

This issue often seems to lead to confusion, because the three levels of requirement evident here are often conflated into two (in the familiar dichotomy of "strong" and "weak" principles or "conclusive" and prima facie principles). With Lyons's weak version of the prima facie or ceteris paribus requirement added to *a* and *b*, we really have three distinct levels of moral requirement. Most minimally, a principle may offer a requirement "ceteris paribus" or "other things being equal" for cases when there is no conflict with other moral considerations. In addition, a principle may specify moral requirements for such cases of conflict but then leave open the question of whether these requirements are, on balance, overriding. Last, a principle may specify a requirement that is, on balance, overriding.

If a principle specifies only the first kind of requirement, it is a *ceteris paribus* principle; if it specifies *both* the first and second, I will say that is specifies *weak actual* requirements. These are weak because they may be overridden, but actual because they do not disappear for cases of conflict.[7] Last, if a principle specifies overriding obligations, its requirements hold in all three cases and I will say that such principles specify *strong actual* obligations. Such obligations are strong because they cannot be overridden and they are actual because they do not disappear in cases of conflict.

---

7. I take this term "actual" from A. John Simmons's useful discussion of prima facie vs. actual requirements, Simmons, *Moral Principles and Political Obligations*, pp. 24–28.

These possibilities, which avoid the ambiguity just noted in the *prima facie* terminology, can be usefully pictured as follows:

	I "Ceteris Paribus" Obligations	II Weak Actual Obligations	III Strong Actual Obligations
1. Required when there are no conflicts	+	+	+
2. Required for cases of conflict	−	+	+
3. Required, on balance, for cases of conflict	−	−	+

I believe that any position which does justice to the complexity of moral conflict will not be limited to principles of type I. Some principles of types II or III, in other words some *actual* obligations (either strong or weak), will have to be admitted. And it is such actual obligation principles that are subject to my argument. If principles of actual obligation are admitted that are both general and positive in form, then the breakdown of individual morality at the large scale is unavoidable. Hence, an important presupposition of the argument which follows is that in addition to specifying obligations which are *general* and *positive*, principles must, in the terminology just discussed, also specify obligations that are *actual*.

One other presupposition needs to be spelled out. In section 4, I alluded to certain "normal conditions" under which the assumptions of the basic structure of individual morality can appropriately be said to apply to any given person.

Apart from these normal conditions, these assumptions may be inappropriate. For example, a person may occupy a particular role or voluntarily undertake special duties. A politician in his role of office, which may be all-consuming, may legitimately find moral questions intruding pervasively. These are, in the technical sense, *special* obligations, rather than *general* ones. They apply only to him because of a role he has undertaken or a burden he has accepted. My argument, on the other hand, will concern the moral condition of ordinary persons and the basic structure of individual morality that normally applies to them. They may, of course, choose to *add* to their obligations if they wish; and these additions will have implications for their moral positions. But for persons with such additional special obligations, these burdens are not morally troubling in the same way as the overload we shall be investigating. Persons in special roles have consented or voluntarily assumed the burdens of office. By contrast, the "breakdown" of the basic structure of individual morality I shall be investigating here occurs without persons voluntarily consenting or adding to their ordinary level of obligation through the occupation of special roles. Our subject, rather, is the breakdown of moral assumptions as they apply generally to ordinary citizens.[8] It is for such ordinary citizens that we commonly assume the acceptability of such a robust zone of indifference. And it is for such ordinary citizens that this assumption breaks down at the large scale when general obligations are also admitted.

It is also possible that the zone of indifference will collapse through special obligations that have not been voluntarily assumed—unusual family obligations, for example. Such a breakdown will not, however, be general. It will apply to particular persons in idiosyncratic situations. Once again, such a case would not affect my argument. For my claim is

8. I assume that in the modern nation-state, any special obligations attached to citizenship are not sufficiently burdensome to overturn the "normal conditions" assumption defined later in this section. For an analysis of the weak demands normally made of democratic citizens, see Dennis F. Thompson, *The Democratic Citizen: Social Science and Democratic Theory in the 20th Century* (Cambridge: Cambridge University Press, 1970).

that we can assume the robustness of the sphere of indifference *apart* from such unusual special obligations (to one's family or attached to one's special role). And these special obligations, I will assume, do not ordinarily overburden the zone of indifference. Hence, under normal conditions most of us do have robust spheres of permissibly free personal choice—spheres vulnerable to the overwhelming pressure of general obligations at the large scale.

The extent to which special obligations intrude abnormally will depend, of course, on the particular details of special obligation principles. I need only make the general assumption that my argument applies for what I shall call "normal conditions," as follows:

> NORMAL CONDITIONS: *A given individual is subject to normal conditions when* special obligations are not so pervasive or demanding as to upset the basic structure.

Some of us may find ourselves in unusual situations where the press of special obligations leads to demands that overwhelm the sphere of indifference. Family obligations may legitimately lead to such burdens under unusual conditions. Or, certain kinds of overwhelming injustice in a particular regime may produce, according to some moral positions, a special obligation to avoid *complicity* with great injustice. Being a citizen of South Africa, for example, may produce special obligations such that maintaining a robust zone of indifference—in blithe disregard for the injustices one was, in a sense, *party to*—would be indefensible. Wartime, similarly, may produce special obligations—either to participate in a just war in defense of one's country or to resist an unjust one—which are so demanding as to upset the basic structure. In such cases, the sphere of indifference may be overwhelmed by special obligations to one's community or to one's country. Furthermore, one may have freely contracted for obligations that may upset the cutoff for heroism. A volunteer for a mission may have a duty (based on his voluntary agreement) for levels of sacrifice that cannot be demanded merely as a matter of general obligation. The assumptions of the basic structure need not apply, for the purposes of our argument, to such cases of overwhelming *special* obligation.

But within the range of "normal conditions" in the sense defined here, the breakdown of the basic structure is more surprising and disturbing. We understand the special burdens of particular roles and we understand the press of obligations based on voluntary agreement. We would not expect the basic structure to apply to such cases. But when the source of overwhelming moral demands cannot be found in such special obligations, then these demands overstep limits that play a crucial role in the structure of our everyday lives—limits that those of us living under "normal conditions" thought were entirely appropriate. In such cases, the vulnerability of the basic structure to breakdown constitutes a challenge to the moral assumptions that underlie the way most of us think and live. Such a general vulnerability to the breakdown of our basic assumptions—within the limits set by the normal conditions just defined—is the subject in the next section.

7. The Implications of Scale

The assumptions introduced here constitute the skeleton of a full-bodied morality. The *unique classification* assumption sets up three distinct spheres of action: (1) indifferent acts, (2) required acts, (3) supererogatory acts. The *robustness of the sphere of indifference* merely establishes that the first category will be a broad one. The *cutoff for heroism* merely establishes a limit to the moral demands required by acts in the second category.

This skeletal structure could be filled out in a great variety of ways. I will not do so, however, because my argument is meant to apply to all the full-bodied moral positions that conform to these assumptions.

The crucial issues revolve around criteria for inclusion in the second category, the sphere of moral requirement, i.e., the sphere containing duties and obligations (both positive and negative). My argument is that if general (positive) obligations are introduced as a basis for the second category, the basic structure defined by the three preceding assumptions becomes vulnerable to breakdown.

In various ways throughout this book, we will investigate this vulnerability as it arises with *increasing scale* in three related senses:

a. *The scale of obligation*: the number of obligation-determining *situations* falling under a given principle of general obligation.

b. *The scale of recipience*: the number of persons who

could be affected by actions falling under a given principle of general obligation.[1]

c. *The scale of action:* the number of moral actors or persons who could perform actions falling under a given principle of general obligation.

Initially, I will formulate the argument in terms of *a.* However, these dimensions are, typically, closely related. In part II, I will focus on two particular principles of general obligation—one for which *a* depends crucially on *b* and the other for which *a* depends crucially on *c.* The first of these, the principle of minimal altruism, leads to breakdowns in the cutoff for heroism and the zone of indifference. The second, the generalization argument, leads to breakdowns in all three assumptions, the cutoff for heroism, the zone of indifference, and the unique classification requirement.[2]

Before proceeding to these patterns of breakdown applying to particular principles, let us establish the general vulnerability of any moral position compatible with the basic structure. I will refer to any violation of the cutoff for heroism or of the robust zone of indifference as an *overload problem.* For an individual is then overburdened with obligations that are either so demanding or so pervasive that too large a measure of sacrifice is demanded (violating the cutoff for heroism) or too large a proportion of his life is morally determined (violating the robust zone of indifference). My general argument is that a vulnerability to overload problems at the large scale is inescapable for any position compatible with the assumptions already defined.

In addition, I will discuss another kind of breakdown, one equally perplexing in its own way. Borrowing from David Lyons, I will refer to any violation of the unique classification

---

1. See n. 3, section 5 above.

2. While I focus on the implications of the generalization argument for the zone of indifference and the unique classification assumption, its relation to the cutoff for heroism is discussed in section 18.

assumption as a non-equivalence problem. The same act is then classified at more than one of the separate moral zones when equivalent moral conclusions were to be expected.[3] Such multiple classifications are troubling because they entail incompatible determinations of what we ought to do, or whether we ought to do anything at all. Depending on the precise formulation of a principle of general obligation, such non-equivalence problems will arise with increases in scale. In part II, I will explore various formulations of the generalization argument and of collective responsibility that lead to such non-equivalence problems at the large scale.

For the moment, however, let us limit our discussion to problems of overload. Some of these overload problems might also be interpreted as non-equivalence problems (in that acts end up being classified as both required and supererogatory), but our primary discussion of non-equivalence problems will come later.

Recall the definitions of the two assumptions in the basic structure that are vulnerable to overload problems:

CUTOFF FOR HEROISM: *Certain levels of sacrifice cannot be morally required of any given individual.*

THE ROBUSTNESS OF THE ZONE OF INDIFFERENCE: *A substantial proportion of any individual's actions fall appropriately within the zone of indifference or permissibly free personal choice.*

Now let us merely assume that any human action must be situated within a spatiotemporal framework such that it takes, at least, some time. Furthermore, we can assume that, however negligible, there is at least some effort, sacrifice, or risk

---

3. Lyons, *Forms and Limits of Utilitarianism*, chapter 3. I have expanded the notion by including conflicts with the supererogatory classification as a ground for non-equivalence. Lyons's central case of non-equivalence—indifference vs. significant (good or bad) consequences—will occupy us in detail in part II.

involved in *any* action. As the number of obligation-determining situations falling under a given principle of general obligation increases, the obligations to which any given person (of at least ordinary capacities) is subject increase so that the time and effort that are morally required accumulate. For any given demarcation for a robust zone of indifference, if the number of obligation-determining situations becomes large enough, the zone will be overwhelmed by enough required acts. Similarly, for any given demarcation for sacrifice, the cutoff will be surpassed when the required effort or the required contributions become great enough. This vulnerability was dramatized in the famine-relief argument when enough minor sacrifices added up to "heroic" proportions.

Because of the way principles of general obligation must be formulated, any given person's theoretical vulnerability to this kind of overload is inescapable. It is important to remember the contrast with special obligations. I can limit my duties resulting from special obligations by not making agreements, promises, or contracts, or by not occupying special roles. Although certain kinship-related obligations are involuntary or quasi-voluntary, under normal conditions they are limited in extent and in any case they are the product of contingent fact. They are limited by definite circumstances and are not vulnerable to the slippery slope affecting general obligations. Every man is not my brother; as a matter of contingent fact, I have, it turns out, only one. The overload from general obligations can be viewed as a result of the kind of moral impartiality that would lead me to treat *every* man *as if* he were my brother. From that perspective, the number of persons who can determine obligations for me is limited only by the numbers who can find themselves in situations relevant to a given principle of general obligation.

A principle of general obligation requires that the obligation would be unchanged if I traded places with any other possible moral agent for the action. Regardless of my identity, my previous history of action, the roles I occupy, my membership in various groups, the obligation for someone to do action X must remain unchanged were I to do it instead of anyone else who might be envisioned as doing it. If there are enough obligation-determining situations corresponding to actions $X_1, X_2, X_3, \ldots, X_N$, when N is large enough, the number of obligations to which I am subject, in this sense, must increase sufficiently to overwhelm any given limits on either time or effort that might be established by either the robust-zone-of-indifference assumption or by the cutoff for heroism.

For this reason, all persons of at least *ordinary* capacities must be vulnerable in theory to a sufficient number of acts required by *positive general obligations* as to overwhelm the limits that, under *normal* conditions, had appeared perfectly appropriate. Because the obligations are positive, they are sufficient to *determine* moral requirements for action.[4] Because the obligations are general, everyone of at least ordinary capacities is, in theory, subject to them. Because the conditions assumed are normal, the persons involved would not already be overloaded with obligations. And because the obligations are *actual*, they determine moral requirements that must be reckoned with even when they conflict with other moral considerations.

Now, we might imagine a possible world—of theoretical interest but no practical relevance—in which, as obligation-determining situations presented themselves, *someone else* always seemed to leap forward, in turn, to do actions X_1, X_2, etc. Even for such a utopian scenario of perfect cooperation, the vulnerability of any given individual to the overload problem is theoretically inescapable—at some point. For as N increases, other persons experience overload. Even if all the others are saints or heroes, at some point, the upper limits of

---

4. Determine requirements, that is, in at least the "weak" sense of *actual* obligations defined in section 6. Whether or not an on-balance requirement for action follows, this is sufficient to take an action out of the sphere of indifference.

possibility must arise if they continue voluntarily taking on enough obligations. At some point, the turn of any given individual must come when it will no longer be true that someone else will do it if he does not.[5] Such considerations about the behavior of others will lead us into a variety of interesting issues in part II, but for now it is worth noting that they do not offer a way out of the general difficulty.

We might also imagine another possible world—also of merely theoretical interest. In this world, morally required actions, though they demand effort, risk, or sacrifice, are always, on balance, rewarding. *Other* benefits always accrue to the agent so that he ends up ahead after discharging his obligations. In this utopian fantasy, morality always pays. In such a case, we would regard overload problems in a different light. For although the robust sphere of indifference would still collapse, in that an agent's actions could be entirely determined for him, the conflicts with the cutoff for heroism could not arise. For in such a world, no matter how many obligations an individual undertook to fulfill, he would end up having benefited, on balance, from his efforts.

Two points need to be made about this possibility. First, the vulnerability of the robustness of the zone-of-indifference assumption is not affected. The general claim—that one or more of the assumptions in the basic structure must be overturned at the large scale—applies even to this imaginary case. Second, the example is interesting because it reveals a presupposition that has, thus far, gone unstated: principles of general obligation are a kind of *moral* principle and for any moral principle, conflicts with self-interest must be theoreti-

---

5. This example reveals why the theoretical difficulty cannot be treated merely as a coordination problem—although such problems have dramatic effects on some particular principles, as we will see in the contrast between utilitarian and Kantian generalization in part II. For some interesting illustrations of coordination problems, see Thomas C. Schelling, *Micromotives and Macrobehavior* (New York: Norton, 1978), and David K. Lewis, *Convention* (Cambridge, Mass.: Harvard University Press, 1969), chapters 1–3.

cally possible. If a principle were formulated so that no conflicts with self-interest were possible, it would be a principle of egoism and not of morality. The possibility of conflicts with self-interest must be admitted if a principle is to be regarded, in the first place, as a moral principle. I will follow a wide variety of theorists in accepting this minimal defining characteristic as one necessary condition for a principle of conduct to be regarded, in the first place, as a moral principle.[6]

Once this theoretical possibility of conflicts with self-interest is admitted, then the principle of general obligation cannot be limited in its application to this fantasy world. It must also be formulated in such a way that it requires obligations for possible cases when they are not, on balance, advantageous or profitable.[7] And, in such a world, the increase of numbers must eventually produce a breakdown, not only in the sphere of indifference, but also in the limits on sacrifice. For possible cases to which the principle must be subject, this breakdown must occur.

For cases in which the breakdown arises because the cutoff for heroism is overwhelmed, it might be said that a simple solution is available; simply regard acts beyond the

6. For example, see Rawls, *Theory of Justice*, on the incompatibility between egoism and the "moral point of view" (section 23): "although egoism is logically consistent and in this sense not irrational, it is incompatible with what we intuitively regard as the moral point of view. The significance of egoism philosophically is not as an alternative conception of right but as a challenge to any such conception" (p. 136). For other approaches to the same conclusion, see Bernard Williams, "Egoism and Altruism," in his *Problems of the Self*, pp. 250–65; and with respect to individual egoism, Brian Medlin, "Ultimate Principles and Ethical Egoism," in David P. Gauthier, ed., *Morality and Rational Self-Interest* (Englewood Cliffs, N.J.: Prentice-Hall, 1970), pp. 56–63. Note that if this requirement were not accepted, this hypothetical example would *still* not count as a counterexample to our central thesis. For conflicts with the robust zone of indifference would not be affected. So long as one or more of the assumptions in the basic structure must break down with increasing scale, the central argument holds.

7. Note how little need be demanded for our argument about the cutoff for heroism to work—as in the weak principle of minimal altruism.

cutoff as supererogatory. But which of our assumptions should have priority? On the one hand, we have the presumption that acts beyond the cutoff for heroism are supererogatory. On the other hand, we have some particular principle of general obligation (whose repeated applications have given rise to the problem). These two assumptions raise an issue of double classification or non-equivalence that cannot simply be solved by definitional fiat. My point, in a sense, is that this problem only arises when a sufficiently large number of individually nonheroic acts add up to heroic proportions. The problem is, itself, a phenomenon of scale in the sense employed here.

Suppose we were to agree that beyond X dollars my contributions to famine relief required by minimal altruism triggered the cutoff for heroism. When I must face the question of whether to give an additional small contribution (say five or ten dollars) to save an additional life, there is considerable moral pressure, from any impartial moral perspective, to *require* that additional small sacrifice as well. If I have to put myself seriously in the place of a starving refugee who might be saved, it is difficult for me to resist *requiring* that any given cutoff for heroism be overwhelmed by yet a further act whose *marginal* sacrifice is clearly nonheroic. So long as there are enough such acts of minimal altruism waiting to be performed, any given effort to reclassify the acts beyond the cutoff as supererogatory must be vulnerable to this kind of moral pressure. I invite the reader to rehearse the arguments for himself as he would conduct them according to the Golden Rule or Rawls's original position or the impartial spectator of the utilitarians. We will return in detail to this problem later. For the moment, it is worth noting that so long as the *marginal* sacrifice of an act is small enough to be nonheroic, we lack a justificatory strategy for calling a halt to the slippery slope. In the case of minimal altruism, the disparity between the effects of a sacrifice that is so small as to be insignificant at the margin for me, but which can produce such enormous good for others, makes the moral pressure to continue giving, when judged from any impartial perspective, very great indeed.

What does this problem have to do with numbers? Only if *enough* individually nonheroic acts are performed by a given individual can this problem arise. Fewer nonheroic acts would not trigger the cutoff. Principles of obligation that do not trigger the cutoff in isolated application must do so, eventually, when applied recurrently to the same individual. This is why our moral conceptions must be refined so as to deal more adequately with the overload problems arising from increasing numbers of relevantly similar cases.

Parellels between this argument and the celebrated "sorites" problem are instructive. First formulated by Eubulides and famous throughout Greek logic,[8] the problem is here

---

8. For historical references to various formulations of the *sorites* problem, see Jon Moline, "Aristotle, Eubulides and the Sorites," *Mind*, July 1969, pp. 393–407. One might also think this argument reminiscent of Zeno's paradoxes. But all four of Zeno's paradoxes turn on *infinite* divisibility, whereas the arguments employed here require only finite divisibility. Compare the infinite divisibility required by Zeno's problem of "Achilles and the Tortoise." Let us say that Achilles begins the race at point A and the Tortoise, with a head start, at point B. During the time it takes Achilles to move from A to B, the Tortoise moves to another point, C. During the time it takes Achilles to move to C, the Tortoise moves to another point, D, etc. No matter how fast Achilles runs, he can never catch the Tortoise because it must always take him *some* time to move to where the Tortoise *was* and the Tortoise, during that time, can always move some distance further ahead, however small. Only when the finite distance actually traveled by the Tortoise over any period is regarded as *infinitely* divisible can we achieve the illusion that there is always a further distance for Achilles to travel in order to catch up. Achilles could clearly overcome a finite number of such step-by-step comparisons merely under the assumption that he travels faster. But an infinite number of such steps leaves him always appearing to be behind. The apparent difficulty in calculating the distances amassed in such an infinite series provides the basis for the paradox.

Note, by contrast, that we have not infinitely divided a finite quantity (say, total sacrifice for famine relief) but have only divided it by a *finite* number (a given number of five-dollar increments). For an interesting discussion of the role of infinity in the various Zeno paradoxes, see Bertrand Russell, "The Problem of Infinity Considered Historically," in Wesley C. Salmon,

unrefined for cases involving a large number of additions of small increments. A small number of additional size increments or a small number of additional sacrifices would not pose the problem. The difficulty in the moral case is that without a refinement in our principles that would permit us to block the inductive premise, we are led to a breakdown in our basic moral conceptions *via* an argument which is logically valid. To deal with this moral parallel to the *sorites*, we must find a justification for blocking the crucial premise. I believe that our moral conceptions are vague enough that at some point it does, indeed, become inappropriate to apply the inductive premise in the moral case, namely: that a minor addition to a nonheroic (or morally acceptable) sacrifice must always be nonheroic (or morally acceptable). But we lack a justificatory strategy for ruling out this crucial inductive premise. And unless the premise is ruled out, the logically valid argument to the conclusion has to be faced (i.e., that the extreme total sacrifice which can result from incremental additions must also be nonheroic or morally acceptable).

It may not matter whether we reformulate our vague conceptions of size. We can simply accept their vague and loose character and block the *sorites* conclusion by refusing to admit the applicability of the inductive premise throughout the range of size variations (or quantity variations for heaps or heads of hair). But in the moral case, we cannot simply accept the vague and loose character of our unrefined moral conceptions. For we are then *still* confronted, in both theory and practice, with the moral problem of how to deal with the additional sacrifices that are apparently required by our unrefined principles. Without a reformulation of our conceptions that would provide a *justification* for barring the inductive premise at some point, our unrefined conceptions drive us to disturbing conclusions that constitute a breakdown in our basic moral assumptions. To say that our unrefined moral conceptions are vulnerable to this parallel of the sorites problem is simply to say that they are vague enough to be inadequate for cases involving a large number of small increments. They must be reformulated if we are to respond adequately to the moral perplexities of real problems of practical reason that arise routinely. This book can be read as an argument that such a reformulation is necessary.

Of course, these moral implications of scale—the breakdown in one or more assumptions of the basic structure—may enter at very different levels for different kinds of acts. The "large scale," in other words, is not to be thought of as any one size (or as beyond any one threshold). In this sense, our earlier analogy with democratic theory should not be taken too literally. It is the simple fact of increasing numbers (in any of our three senses) and not the more specific distinction between the city-state and the nation-state that supports the analogy. Problems of scale in my sense could certainly occur in a city-state. They are, however, more obvious in a nation-state and even more obvious in an interconnected world community. Another comparison might also be useful. Economists have identified the phenomenon of "effects of scale" across very different kinds of economic activity, even though these effects of scale may become important at points that vary greatly from one industry to the next. Similarly, the moral effects of scale that concern us—namely, the breakdown in the basic structure of morality when the number of cases falling under a principle of general obligation becomes large enough—may enter at quite different points for different kinds of acts under different evaluative and factual assumptions. However, the link between this breakdown and increasing numbers should be recognizable across these differences. The central point is that *any* moral position committed to the stated assumptions—for which, within some range of cases those assumptions can be maintained—will become vulnerable to breakdown when the number of cases becomes large enough.

At first glance, this general vulnerability might appear to be of merely theoretical interest. The real issue, it might be said, is whether this abstract *possibility* of breakdown arises for real cases. My argument in part II is directed at this issue. For there, I will argue that this kind of breakdown does not merely arise for some imaginary cases affecting any possible moral position committed to the stated assumptions. Rather, it arises for real cases affecting the moral positions to which many of us are deeply committed. These problems are a common source of perplexity in our actual lives, whenever we bother to think about moral issues involving large numbers.

PART II:

Applications

8. Minimal Altruism

A critic might attempt to trivialize the argument of part I by saying that all I have shown is that "when there are too many obligations, there are, indeed, too many obligations." The significance of the argument just completed, however, revolves around two points left out of this caricature: (a) the argument reveals the assumptions which render us vulnerable to "too many obligations" and (b) it clarifies the price we would have to pay for "too many obligations." If we were to have a coherent moral position at what I have called the "large-scale," we would have to give up either (1) one or more parts of the basic structure of individual morality or (2) our commitment to general obligations. We will return to this basic dilemma in part III.

In the meantime, we will focus on particular principles of general obligation that render us vulnerable to breakdowns in the basic structure. Any such principle exposes us to the theoretical problem if enough relevant cases happen to arise in the world. Regardless of how steadfastly we refuse to undertake new obligations, we are vulnerable in this way to general obligations (as compared to special ones). But the empirical circumstances under which these difficulties arise will vary markedly with the precise formulation of a principle of general obligation and with the precise interpretation of assumptions in the basic structure (particularly, the cutoff for heroism and the robust sphere of indifference). My argument in part II is that particular principles that many of us find compelling are vulnerable to these difficulties, not merely for some *possible* cases, but for *actual* cases that arise routinely in our daily lives. These theoretical perplexities are, in other words, of immediate practical relevance.

In order to establish such a claim, I must discuss particular substantive principles. I have picked some familiar ones which, I believe, have broad appeal. If, however, I have left out the reader's own particular substantive positions, then I invite him to envision how the general argument of part I would apply to them. If they conform to the basic structure, then the breakdown is theoretically unavoidable. I would be surprised, in addition, if any such positions escaped practical vulnerability for real cases. For virtually any plausible moral position, numbers large enough to yield problems of overload (and perhaps also problems of non-equivalence) are a commonplace phenomenon. But as we have noted, this issue is partly empirical and must be explored in detail for each moral position.

The principles we will investigate vary in how they take account of the availability of others to perform the same action. Some notions of obligation are defined *independently* of the behavior of others. For such a principle, in order to determine whether person A should do action X, I need not know anything about the availability of others (B, C, D, etc.) to do X. Other principles, by contrast, define obligations so that they are *dependent* on the behavior of others. For such principles, I *do* need to know about the availability of one or more others (B, C, D, etc.) to do action X before I can determine whether A should do X. Two common principles that define obligations "dependently" in this sense are *generalization arguments* (asking us to envision the consequences of "everyone doing the same") and principles that include riders for *collective responsibility* (where A might not be held responsible for doing X when enough others were also available to do X).

The "independent" principles are, in important respects, simpler. I will begin with an independent principle and then,

later in part II, move to incorporate the complications resulting from the behavior of others for "dependent" principles.

The principle of minimal altruism alluded to earlier is an
"independent" principle that offers a good starting point. It is
general and positive in form and it should have, I believe,
broad appeal. Most importantly, it reveals our vulnerability to
breakdowns in the basic structure for some real and disturbing cases. Let us define this principle as follows:

MINIMAL ALTRUISM: *If a person knows that he can prevent
great harm, such as the loss of a human life, he is morally
obligated to do so if the costs to him (and to anyone else)
are minor.*

In this weak form, requiring sacrifice only when the cost
is minor, the principle is very difficult to argue against. Relin-
quishing such minimal requirements for mutual aid would
result in a very great revision in our common moral conceptions.

Consider this example proposed by Brian Barry. Several
people are stranded on a rock. They will drown when the tide
rises unless they are rescued. If a man happened along in a
boat and the task was sufficiently easy, most of us would, I believe, agree with Barry and "treat the man as a moral leper if
he failed to rescue the people—the man happened to be pass-
ing the rock anyway, the sea was calm, and he could have
taken the stranded people off at almost no inconvenience or
risk to himself."[1] I think if it were even one person stranded
on the rock, we would react in the same way. On the other
hand, as Barry notes, if the risks were sufficiently great (the
sea was stormy, etc.), we might not blame the man in the boat
if he failed to attempt a rescue. But if the costs can be rea-

---

1. Brian Barry, "And Who Is My Neighbor?" *Yale Law Journal* 88
(1979): 629–58. The quotation is from page 638.

sonably expected to be trivial, then the case falls under a principle whose demands are as minimal as the one just proposed.

In his studies of the psychology of moral reasoning, Lawrence Kohlberg poses the dilemma of "Heinz" whose wife is dying of a terrible disease. A druggist has invented a drug that would save her, but he insists on an exorbitant price. When Heinz exhausts every other possible means of obtaining the drug, he steals it from the druggist.

Many of the responses Kohlberg classifies as "higher" or more developed would require that Heinz steal the drug not only for his beloved wife but also for an acquaintance or a stranger who has no special claim on him. The most adequate moral position, according to Kohlberg, requires that rights and duties be completely "correlative." Each person's right to life defines a corresponding *duty* for everyone that he be saved.[2]

Such a position obviously goes far beyond the requirements of our "minimal" principle. For stealing the drug can be expected to involve substantial sacrifice (a prison term, etc.). Let us alter the situation so that the sacrifice is clearly trivial. Suppose that Heinz and his wife have raised the money for the drug and they need only to arrive at the druggist's laboratory within a few hours for the treatment to be given in time. They are hopelessly lost and come upon you on the road. You can show them the way by taking a few minutes from your leisurely stroll in the countryside. Would it not be morally indefensible for you to refuse? Could any of us defend rejection of this minimal principle?

It should be obvious that a wide variety of moral positions would be committed *at least* to this kind of altruism. For example, this principle follows immediately from utilitarianism for utilitarianism is committed to a strong doc-

---

2. Lawrence Kohlberg, "Justice as Reversibility," in Laslett and Fishkin, eds., *Philosophy, Politics and Society,* Fifth Series, pp. 257–72.

trine of "negative responsibility"—the consequences of failures to act must be counted in the same way as those of positive actions. If the loss of a human life has great negative disutility (at least to the person who is about to die) and if the sacrifice is minor, then the prospective benefits of action clearly outweigh the costs. This result follows, not only when the benefits and costs are calculated in terms of pleasure and pain, but also when they are defined in terms of other reasonable versions of consequentialism.

This position can also be found in Kantian morality. Kant himself appears to endorse such a principle. In the *Groundwork of the Metaphysics of Morals* Kant cites the case of a prosperous man who "sees that others (whom he could help) have to struggle with great hardships." Such a man asks: "What concern of mine is it? Let each one be as happy as heaven wills, or as he can make himself; I will not take anything from him or even envy him; but to his welfare or to his assistance in time of need, I have no desire to contribute."[3]

Kant argues that while it is possible that this maxim could be adopted as a universal law of nature, we could not *will* it to hold universally: "For a will which resolved this would conflict with itself, since instances can often arise in which he would need the love and sympathy of others, and in which he would have robbed himself, by such law of nature springing from his own nature, of all hope of the aid he desires."[4]

Whatever we think of Kant's attempt here to provide a rational grounding for the principle, it is clear that Kant is committed to *at least* the degree of altruism defined by our minimal principle. Fried interprets these passages as requiring more than this, more than the principle that "we have the duty to relieve the fortuitous distress of another when we can

---

3. Immanuel Kant, *Groundwork of the Metaphysic of Morals*, translated and analyzed by H. J. Paton (New York: Harper Torchbooks, 1956), pp. 90–91 (page 56 in Kant's 2nd ed).
    4. Ibid.

do so without great inconvenience."⁵ But the test is, admittedly, ambiguous about how much sacrifice we can be morally obligated to incur.

Richards, in his reconstruction of Kantian morality, offers a similar principle: "if a person X encounters another person Y, where X may, at only slight cost to himself, relieve Y's great pain or injury, or aid Y in averting such pain, injury or even death, then X is to give such relief and aid, assuming that Y does not voluntarily and rationally refuse it."⁶ Once again, the principle of obligation is conditioned by the proviso "at only slight cost to himself." Such a minimal requirement would be agreed to by a wide range of theorists.

The only prominent exception of which I am aware is Robert Nozick. The doctrine of rights developed in *Anarchy, State and Utopia* provides for an absolute prohibition against "boundary crossings" but no condemnation for failures to act (unless obligations to act were freely contracted for). The rich have no obligations to contribute to the poor for famine relief. It would be impermissible for the state to force them to do so—for such forced redistribution would violate their rights.⁷

---

5. Fried, *Right and Wrong*, p. 115. See the discussion of "imperfect duties" in section 19 below.

6. Richards, *Theory of Reasons*, p. 187.

7. Robert Nozick, *Anarchy, State and Utopia* (New York: Basic Books, 1974), especially chapter 3. I pursue this interpretation of Nozick in more detail in my *Tyranny and Legitimacy*, chapter 9. Peter Singer offers (without citation) a quite different reading of Nozick, which might possibly insulate him from this kind of objection: "A theory of property rights can insist on our *right* to retain wealth without pronouncing on whether the rich *ought* to give to the poor. Nozick, for example, rejects the use of compulsory means like taxation to redistribute income, but suggests that we can achieve the ends we deem morally desirable by voluntary means. So Nozick would reject the claim that rich people have an 'obligation' to give to the poor, in so far as this implies that the poor have a right to our aid, but might accept that giving is something we ought to do and failing to give, though within one's rights, is wrong, for rights is not all there is to ethics" (Singer, *Practical Ethics*, p. 173.). Singer seems to be claiming that Nozick provides a basis for other moral requirements (and not merely supererogatory judgments) than those derived from his theory of rights. I cannot find a basis in the text for this position and

Although Nozick would not be committed to our minimal principle, he realizes that this position falls outside the general consensus: "many persons will reject our conclusions instantly, knowing they don't *want* to believe anything so apparently callous toward the needs and suffering of others."[8] Elsewhere, I have argued that it is this very "callousness" in his fundamental assumptions (a callousness that goes so far as to deny what we have called minimal altruism) which renders Nozick's entire theory vulnerable to some decisive objections.[9]

Of course, I have no need to argue that this principle of general obligation—or any of the others to be discussed here—will be accepted by everyone. It is, however, advocated by a wide range of theorists who otherwise disagree sharply. Those of us who fall within this consensus must take account of the implications of scale to which this widely appealing principle is subject. It is to those implications that we now turn.

---

believe that my own view conforms to the standard interpretation. See, for example, David Lyons's observation in his review of Nozick that "no objections from outside the realm of rights are ever suggested." David Lyons, "Rights Against Humanity," *The Philosophical Review* 85 (1976): 208–15; the quotation is from page 214. If Singer is correct, then the position that *would* result from a limitation of moral requirements to rights in Nozick's sense will serve to illustrate my argument (for the kind of position that would be compatible with a denial of positive general obligations). Whether Nozick actually subscribes to this position does not, in the end, matter for the point developed here.

8. Nozick, *Anarchy, State and Utopia*, p. ix.

9. Fishkin, *Tyranny and Legitimacy*, chapter 9.

9. The Famine Relief Argument

According to the cutoff for heroism, there must be limits on the sacrifice that can be demanded of any individual as a matter of obligation. For example, although we might be morally required to give to famine relief, it would be beyond the call of duty for us to give so much that we starved ourselves down to the same level as those we were trying to save. Peter Singer, in a provocative essay, denies this conclusion. He argues that we are obligated to give until we reach the "level of marginal utility," i.e., the level at which a dollar sacrificed does as much harm to us as it does good for a starving Bengali refugee. On Singer's view, such sacrifices would not only be admirable; they are also morally *required* of us all.[1]

Given the assumptions adopted here, we cannot, as a matter of obligation, be required to go so far as Singer demands. Although it would be admirable or virtuous of anyone to do so, all of us who contribute less cannot be morally wrong. We cannot, in other words, be morally *required* to be heroes. The fact that we seem to be led to such a conclusion is an indication that something has gone wrong: this is an instance of a family of problematical cases that arise only at the large scale.

Singer's argument is based on a slightly stronger premise

---

1. This is the implication of the "strong principle" that Singer endorses: "The strong version, which required us to prevent bad things from happening unless in doing so we would be sacrificing something of comparable moral significance, does seem to require reducing ourselves to the level of marginal utility. I should also say that the strong version seems to me to be the correct one." Singer, "Famine, Affluence and Morality," p. 33.

than the one we discussed in the last section. His assumption is that: "if it is in our power to prevent something very bad from happening, without thereby sacrificing anything of comparable moral importance, we ought, morally, to do it." This assumption is stronger than our own assumption of minimal altruism, because it would require sacrifices not only when they are minor but also when they are significant—but still not of "comparable moral importance" to the harm that is to be prevented. Singer's claim is that, for most of us, this degree of sacrifice would not be reached until one had reduced one's self "to very near the material circumstances of a Bengali refugee."[2]

Singer also considers a weaker premise—one he considers to be less adequate than the stronger one—"if it is in our power to prevent something bad from happening, without thereby sacrificing anything morally significant, we ought, morally, to do it."[3] This principle is closely related to our own principle of minimal altruism. It is less demanding than Singer's "strong" principle, because it would not require us to act if we would be "sacrificing *anything* morally significant." Singer's position, however, is that this "weak" principle is inadequate, because it would probably not require an average citizen in the Western developed countries to sacrifice more than about 10 percent of his income.[4] The weak principle, he concludes, is "too weak because it makes it too easy for the duty of benevolence to be avoided."[5]

Yet, I wish to claim that once the implications of scale are taken into account, even this apparently "weak" principle

---

2. Ibid., pp. 23, 33.

3. Ibid., p. 23.

4. Peter Singer, "Reconsidering the Famine Relief Argument," in Peter G. Brown and Henry Shue, eds., *Food Policy* (New York: The Free Press, 1977), pp. 36–49; this point is made on page 49.

5. Peter Singer, "Postscript" to "Famine, Affluence and Morality," in William Aiken and Hugh LaFollette, eds., *World Hunger and Moral Obligation* (Englewood Cliffs, N.J.: Prentice-Hall, 1977), pp. 33–36. The quotation is from p. 36.

can require sacrifices so great that they can only be called heroic. At the large scale, this kind of principle has implications more startling than Singer imagines. The kind of perplexity it produces is part of a family of cases that can only arise when the numbers are large enough.

We have already seen the difficulty. If every small contribution to famine relief will save a human life or prevent other serious harm (for example, by facilitating the delivery of surplus foodstuffs to those facing imminent starvation), then I am obligated by the principle of minimal altruism to give—and to continue giving—until the *marginal* sacrifice involved in any individual act of giving is more than minor. The disparity in affluence between the developed countries and the world's poor is so enormous that an American citizen of average means, such as this author, could give half his income—and it would still be the case that an *additional* small contribution would be a minor sacrifice. If I were reduced to half my present (junior faculty) salary, I could still afford to give five more dollars. What would I do with five dollars? Go to the movies? Pay for part of my new pair of sunglasses? Buy a paperback book? A further sacrifice of five dollars at the margin (if it had any noticeable effect on my life at all even at that level of income) would only affect such minor *discretionary* expenditures. What are any of these benefits compared to the good that can be done for an unknown starving person by contributions to famine relief?

The difficulty, of course, in consistently applying this principle is that we would be led, step by step, to sacrifices of heroic proportions. If a large enough number of acts fall under this principle of minimal altruism, then they accumulate to sacrifices which, in total, should be regarded as heroic under the cutoff for heroism. We thus come to classify the same acts as obligatory, on the one hand, and heroic or supererogatory, on the other.

It should be obvious that if there were only a *few* such sacrifices, this conflict of assumptions would not arise. For the principle of minimal altruism can only require minor sacrifices and a few such minor sacrifices cannot add up to heroic proportions. Only if the number of such cases becomes large enough can we arrive at this conflict where the same acts are classified as both obligatory and beyond the call of duty.

Now it might be objected that this argument takes no account of distance. Effects on persons far away are counted in the same way as effects on those close by. Of course, we habitually do concern ourselves more with those near to us. And there are often good reasons for us to do so. Proximity provides opportunities for action, it lowers the costs of action, and it increases our confidence about the effects of those actions.

Yet, if cases involving far-away persons share these same characteristics, then surely the mere fact of distance provides no reason for ignoring the effects. Suppose there were a button in my office which, if pushed, would cause some unknown, particular person on the other side of the world to be instantaneously blown up. Surely, if I pushed this button in full knowledge of the consequences, that would be regarded as murder just as surely as if I had caused that person to be blown up in front of me. The distance and its attendant anonymity make no difference to our evaluation of this act of *commission*. Why should it make any difference to an act of *omission* (such as the consequences of failing to give to famine relief)? If we were equally confident about the results, the distance, by itself, should make no difference.

But the result of consistently applying our principle of minimal altruism to a large enough number of cases is that the sphere of obligation intrudes not only on the sphere of supererogation (because we become obligated beyond the call of duty) but also on the sphere of indifference. For the disparity is so great between the level of affluence we take for granted and the level of poverty common in the third (and fourth) world, that we can—in incurring a host of minor sacrifices in time and effort as well as in money and resources—

always be required to do more. Even so weak a principle as minimal altruism would have a pervasive effect on our everyday lives. What sphere of our private life could steadfastly withstand responsibility for *omissions* to work for famine relief, population control, and a host of other immediate causes? We are easily led to the conclusion that a vast reform is *required* in the entire way of life we take for granted.

Something like this kind of calculation stands behind the uneasiness that Michael Harrington expresses (in a thoughtful and ambitious book, *The Vast Majority: A Journey to the World's Poor*) about the apparently trivial problem of whether to take his tennis racket on a visit to India. In offering us some "autobiographical notes," he claims to be "representative" of most of his readers, "unheroic, immersed in Western comforts, no Saint Francis of Assisi." In confronting Third World poverty, he confesses, "I am a contradictory, compromised and somewhat baffled person." On his way to an academic conference: "I could not see myself boarding a plane, carrying a tennis racket, on my way to what could be fore me the heart of darkness, the horror." Once there (without his tennis racket), he was haunted by unending lines of beggars: "I have tried every strategy I know for dealing with them—to give, which brings a new line of supplicants; to say no, which means that they would follow, pleading in a kind of singsong chant." After escaping into a plush hotel, he felt trapped by "that militant, counterrevolutionary poverty that, on its knees to the West, waited just outside the door, and frightened and sickened me and reached out to my heart."[6]

Harrington's uneasiness about his tennis racket is emblematic of the difficulty any of us would face in justifying almost any particular normal activity within the sphere of indifference—if we had to justify it in the face of the good we could be doing *instead* if we were willing to devote ourselves

6. Michael Harrington, *The Vast Majority: A Journey to the World's Poor* (New York: Simon and Shuster, 1977), pp. 30, 56, 70.

wholeheartedly to the effort. This kind of reasoning, if applied systematically, would force us, step by step, to renounce our entire way of life. Yet, on the assumptions stated here, we cannot be *obligated* to do so, because such a renunciation would, in its *total* effect upon us, constitute a sacrifice great enough to violate the cutoff for heroism. In addition, anyone conforming to such requirements would clearly have renounced his (normally) robust sphere of indifference. His entire way of life would be structured so as to conform to these (positive) moral requirements. Both the cutoff for heroism and the robust sphere of indifference must become overloaded for this kind of case.

But in order to defend the claim that we are *not* obligated to give up our entire way of life, must we then defend the notion that the world is in a morally preferable state: (a) when we live in comparative luxury and frivolity while some people starve, as opposed to (b) when we efficaciously sacrifice as much as we can—in time, effort, and resources—to ensure that no one, or as few persons as possible, is starving? If placing a limit on what can be demanded of any *individual* required the defense of such a moral claim (that *a* was better than *b*) then, I believe such a limit would be indefensible. We would then each be morally *required* to give up our entire way of life and devote ourselves full time to the amelioration of world poverty, disease, and overpopulation. However, such a conclusion would conflate a question about moral *states of the world* with a question about what individuals (as opposed to groups or nations) should be morally *required* to do about affecting those states of the world. It would force each of us, as individuals, to shoulder the entire burden of *any* difference we can affect in states of the world. This is a recognizable moral position—a demanding version of consequentialism that we might call *strict consequentialism*.

Strict consequentialism requires that we do *whatever* actions are open to us that will bring about better states of the world, and that we avoid *whatever* actions are open to us that will bring about worse states of the world. This is a more demanding doctrine than other familiar consequentialist positions. For we can define a broader notion that might be called *weak consequentialism,* such that if we are morally required to do (or not to do) X it can only be because a better (or worse) state of the world would result. However, this does not mean that we are morally required to do (or not do) *whatever* will bring about better (or worse) states of the world. An act might, for example, be beyond the call of duty in the amount of sacrifice it involved. Even though a better state of the world would result, we might not be required to do it. However, it could still be true that for every act we *are* required to perform (or not to perform) there corresponds a correct claim about the better (or worse) state of the world that would result. This kind of limitation for acts beyond the call of duty would be compatible with the weak consequentialist position—although not with the more demanding doctrine of strict consequentialism.[7]

This distinction has some very important implications. For if morality must be *strictly* consequentialist, then we immediately arrive at a dilemma. Either the *a* alternative just mentioned is a morally better state of the world (the state in which we continue our way of life and others starve) or *b* is really better, and we are then obligated to do what we can to see that as few starve as possible. When followed consistently the latter alternative would lead us to an apparently supererogatory level of sacrifice (requiring that we all devote

---

7. The term "consequentialism" was coined by G. E. M. Anscombe in her 1958 article, "Modern Moral Philosophy," reprinted in Thomson and Dworkin, eds., *Ethics,* pp. 186–210. See also the discussions in Brian Barry, "And Who Is My Neighbor?" and Bernard Williams, "A Critique of Utilitarianism," in J. J. C. Smart and Bernard Williams, *Utilitarianism: For and Against* (Cambridge: Cambridge University Press, 1973), pp. 77–150, especially pp. 82–92; and Charles Fried, *Right and Wrong,* chapter 1. The problem of overload for what I have called a strictly consequentialist version of utilitarianism is discussed in Anthony Quinton, *Utilitarian Ethics* (New York: St. Martin's, 1973), pp. 46–47.

ourselves full-time to good causes), but perhaps that amount of sacrifice should be required and not viewed as discretionary.

Strict consequentialism starkly reduces the morally defensible alternatives. In a disturbing article on famine relief, Jan Narveson arrives at the following dilemma on the basis of this kind of assumption:

> Either we literally do everything we can: which, in the case of many of us, would mean not ten dollars or two or three percent of our incomes, but probably sixty or seventy percent. Or we make a judgment that *the importance of the kind of life we have set out to live is greater than the amount of suffering preventable by depriving ourselves of the means to live it.*[8]

Narveson takes the admittedly "heretical" position that there is more to be said for the latter position than might be imagined: If one properly weighs the quality as well as the quantity of life, it is arguable that the status quo is, in fact, a preferable state of the world. He gives us an "aesthete" who reasons:

> And if it came to a choice between enabling some few to enjoy such an existence even though many elsewhere should perish from want, and of just keeping the latter alive at the cost of forever keeping the good life from the grasp of the former when we know it could be done, I for one should unhesitatingly opt for the first.[9]

I believe that the position of Narveson's "aesthete," although coherent, is morally indefensible. The world is not in a morally preferable state when some people suffer avoidable starvation while others do nothing about it and continue lives

---

8. Jan Narveson, "Aesthetics, Charity, Utility and Distributive Justice," in *The Monist* 56 (1962): 527–51. The quotation is from p. 551.
9. Ibid., p. 538.

of comparative luxury, listening to opera—or writing philosophy—whereas they might otherwise be working full-time to alleviate suffering somewhere in the world.

But to say that the world could be in a better state is *not* to say that we are, by that fact alone, required to drop everything in order to bring that better state about. For one of our basic assumptions throughout has been that there are *limits* on what can morally be required of individuals. These limits find expression in the notion that there is a cutoff for heroism. Accepting this assumption is, by itself, a departure from strict consequentialism (although it is compatible with the more general consequentialist position just defined). For it means there are acts that would bring about better states of the world which we are not *required* to perform (because they would involve too great a sacrifice). Strict consequentialism would lead to Narveson's dilemma; other moral positions, including other, weaker versions of consequentialism, would not.

In other words, we need not argue, as Narveson has tried to, that the world is overall in a preferable state when we live the good life while others (somewhere in the world) starve. We could admit that the world would overall be a better place if we (individually and/or collectively) gave up our way of life and heroically devoted ourselves to the relief of poverty, disease, and overpopulation. However, this admission does not yield the conclusion that we are morally required to make the sacrifice. If I could save Y's life by reaching into a machine and having my arm cut off, I might admit that the overall state of the world would be better (1) if Y lived and J. F. was armless, as opposed to (2) if Y died and J. F. had both of his arms. Yet, this admission does not directly yield the conclusion that I would be *obligated* to bring about (1) rather than (2).

A premise of this book is that there are limits on what can be demanded of individuals. Of course, this does not mean that we need do nothing at all. I believe we are all obligated to make *some* sacrifices to help alleviate the suffering and distress of others. I wish to affirm this clearly. My argument is that special difficulties arise in determining how much we are obligated to do at the large scale. We face special difficulties when the numbers are large enough, because assumptions that cannot otherwise conflict lead to conflicting conclusions at the large scale. This is why these choices are not only emotionally agonizing but also perplexing from the standpoint of moral and political theory.

At the large scale, we cannot remain simultaneously committed to two assumptions that have a prominent place in our common moral conceptions: (1) the extremely weak principle of general obligation I have called "minimal altruism," and (2) the assumption (from the basic structure) that there is a "cutoff for heroism." One or both of these notions must be reformulated if they are to be applied consistently at the large scale.

However they are reformulated, an adequate response to the following dilemma will be necessary: On the one hand, if we respond affirmatively to every appeal supported by the principle of minimal altruism, we will find ourselves obligated to a level of cumulative sacrifice that can only be called heroic. On the other hand, if at any earlier point we respond negatively, then we must have some justification for denying aid to someone when that aid would save a life (or prevent very great harm) when we could do so at insignificant cost.

I must confess that I do not have a defensible solution to this dilemma. My concern has been, rather, to show that it can only arise when the number of cases falling under these principles is large enough.

10. Collective Responsibility

There is another issue raised by the famine-relief problem: Does my responsibility for not doing X vary according to whether others are similarly placed? Consider the Kitty Genovese case referred to earlier:

> Kitty Genovese is set upon by a maniac as she returns home from work at 3 A.M. Thirty-eight of her neighbors in Kew Gardens come to their windows when she cries out in terror; none comes to her assistance even though her stalker takes over half an hour to murder her. No one even so much as calls the police. She dies.[1]

Is the responsibility of each person lessened by the fact that each knows he is not the only one who could call the police? Are expectations about the behavior of others relevant to our evaluation of the act? This is an issue that, as we shall see, arises for the generalization argument as well. One definable view of responsibility would leave it unaffected, when shared. As Nozick expresses it, "Responsibility is not a bucket in which less remains when some is apportioned out."[2] Singer takes this position with respect to omissions for famine relief. There is no significant difference, he claims, between the case in which I share responsibility among "millions" and the case "in which I am the only person who can

---

1. Bibb Latané and John M. Darley, *The Unresponsive Bystander: Why Doesn't He Help?* (Englewood Cliffs, N.J.: Prentice-Hall, 1970), p. 1.
2. Nozick, "Anarchy, State and Utopia," p. 130.

prevent something very bad from occurring."[3] Let us call this the *invariant view* of collective responsibility for omissions. It does not vary when it is more widely shared.

A second view of responsibility would regard it as *diminishing* when it is more widely shared. On this view, if the Kitty Genovese murder had been witnessed by a thousand persons, their individual responsibility for failing to alert the police would be less than in the case of only thirty-eight witnesses. Furthermore, if there had been only one witness, his individual responsibility would be far greater, on this view, than in the cases where it is more widely shared. One reason, of course, is that his omission, singlehandedly, ensures that she is cut off from all reasonable hope of assistance.

To take an example at the opposite extreme, suppose that the tragic case of Kitty Genovese were witnessed, not by thirty-eight persons, but by ten million. Perhaps through some bizarre accident it has been televised live to millions. Would we hold each of the ten million viewers responsible in the same way as we held the thirty-eight neighbors responsible?

My point is that according to this second, *diminishing* view of collective responsibility, there must come a point, surely, where the level of responsibility for an omission—when widely enough shared—becomes insignificant. By this I mean that it no longer corresponds to the moral significance we attach to acts in the obligatory category. I am not advocating this diminishing view; however, adopting it would imply an additional kind of perplexity at the large scale.

For we would normally assume that if we are obligated to do X, our responsibility for not doing X (if we fail to do it) must be morally significant. However, only if this responsibility for an omission is shared by a large enough number could it be eventually trivialized by the diminishing view. Only then could we be *obligated* to perform an action (according to

---

3. Singer, "Famine, Affluence and Morality," pp. 24–25.

a principle such as minimal altruism) while our responsibility, if we fail to perform it, would be insignificant. Only then could we easily accomplish something so important as saving a life—but not bear significant responsibility if we failed to do so.

In other words, an additional conflict arises at the large scale on this view. For the diminishing view of collective responsibility would not hold us strictly to task for equally sharing an omission among, say, ten million television viewers, whereas it might hold us strictly responsible if we were one of Kitty Genovese's thirty-eight neighbors. The "ought" when widely enough shared might be viewed as the discretionary "ought" of the supererogatory category (it would be good of us to do it but not wrong if we did not). However, since we can single-handedly, and at trivial cost, intervene successfully we are—by a principle such as minimal altruism—obligated to do so. On this view, the act is not discretionary but rather is morally required. This kind of conflicting moral classification or "non-equivalence" can only arise if our responsibility for the omission is shared widely enough, i.e., if enough others are situated with respect to the act in the same way as we are. The unique classification assumption would be violated for such a case—but only when the collective responsibility was shared widely enough.

There is a third view of collective responsibility that is, I believe, more adequate than either the invariant view or this diminishing view. The difficulty with the invariant view is that it is insensitive to our special responsibility at the lower end. When we are, for example, the only one who could help, we have an especially severe responsibility if we fail to do so. On the other hand, the difficulty with the diminishing view is that it would allow responsibility to decrease merely as a function of how it is shared. This leaves it insensitive to another factor that seems relevant for this kind of case—namely, our estimation of what difference our act is likely to make after we take into account the behavior of others.

Consider this example of Feinberg's:

Suppose a man swimming off a public beach that lacks a professional lifeguard shouts for help in a voice audible to a group of one thousand accomplished swimmers lolling on the beach; and yet no one moves to help him, and he is left to drown.[4]

The difficulty, of course, is that if everyone felt a duty to rescue the drowning man—and if everyone acted on that duty—the results might be worse than if no one did. For a chaotic hoard of swimmers, getting in each other's way, perhaps creating more accidents, would result.

Feinberg's solution for this case is that:

each has a duty to attempt rescue so long as no more than a few others have already begun their efforts. In short, everyone should use his eyes and his common sense and cooperate as best he can. If no one makes any motion at all, it follows that no one has done his best within the limits imposed by the situation, and *all* are subject at least to blame.[5]

I would interpret Feinberg's suggestion as permitting a potential rescuer to calculate the likely effects of his action in a causal context that permits him to take into account the likely effects of the behavior of others (if these can be reasonably estimated). In the Kitty Genovese case, of course, the neighbors (unlike Feinberg's swimmers) are ignorant of the behavior of others. But if we permit them to make reasonable suppositions about the likely effects of the behavior of others, then they might assume that as the numbers increase it is more likely that at least *someone* will act. So while they might each be significantly responsible in a group of thirty-eight (because there is still a substantial risk that no one else will

---

4. Feinberg, *Doing and Deserving*, p. 243.
5. Ibid., p. 244.

have called), a person might be forgiven the assumption that in a group of ten million persons watching television, at least one person will have called the police.[6] If this supposition is permitted, then the inference becomes reasonable that one is not significantly responsible for failing to telephone because one's call could not have been reasonably expected to make any difference (because many others out of the ten million could surely be expected to do so). In other words, on this view, inferences about the behavior of others are permissible in order to determine the benchmark for measuring the *difference* one's action can be expected to make.

Let us call this third view of collective responsibility for omissions the *reasonably expectable difference* view. We calculate the effects of our action in the causal context defined by reasonable inferences about the effects of others' behavior. We then determine the difference our act can be expected to make. We are not obligated to join the rescue of the swimmers if we can see that there are already enough (or more than enough others) attempting the rescue. In that causal context, our action is not expected to make any difference; in fact, it might be expected to complicate matters. But if, on the other hand, we are among the thirty-eight witnesses to Kitty Genovese, we can expect that our actions might very well make a difference. We cannot then be confident that someone else has already called. If I am, furthermore, the *only* witness, I can be quite confident that my action will make a difference. This formulation captures the more urgent obligation in such a case.

---

6. This supposition is compatible with the finding of Latané and Darley that, as group size increases, the likelihood of any *given* bystander's responding decreases. It is possible for the likelihood that *someone* out of the whole group will respond to *increase* with group size, whereas the likelihood that any *particular* person will call decreases—in part, because he is more sure that someone else in the large group has probably done it anyway. See Latané and Darley, *The Unresponsive Bystander,* chapters 10 and 11 for the effects of group size and for the diffusion of responsibility.

By contrast, if we can assume that at least *some* others will call in a group of ten million, then the action is rendered discretionary rather than obligatory because it cannot be expected to make a significant difference. This is not to deny that it would be a good or morally admirable thing to do. It is to say, however, that the likely effects of the action are no longer of sufficient significance that we can be blamed if we fail to act.

It is worth emphasizing that this third view of collective responsibility, though it resolves some of these anomalies, leaves the moral problem posed by famine relief entirely unaffected. We face the same dilemma as before, for in that case, each additional contribution can be expected to affect an additional recipient. So long as it can be reasonably expected that we will not run out of poor people needing assistance, our contributions can be expected to make a significant difference. In other words, the shared character of the responsibility does not affect the obligatory character of the act. After we incorporate reasonable suppositions about the contributions of others, we can still expect that our own contributions will do some good. And by this third view of collective responsibility, we must be responsible for the *difference* that our actions can be expected to make.

Whether or not I am right in claiming that this third view of collective responsibility is more adequate than the other two, problematical cases arise at the large scale. On the *diminishing* view, responsibility for the omission falls under a discretionary 'ought' when it is widely enough shared—even though actual performance of the action would still be obligatory by the principle of minimal altruism. Since the 'ought' cannot be both discretionary (supererogatory) and required, this is the same kind of "non-equivalence" (between supererogation and obligation) encountered earlier.

And as we have already seen in detail, on both Singer's *invariant* view and on the proposal offered here, our duties for famine relief become problematical at the large scale. For on either view, the act of contributing appears both obligatory and heroic—it is both something we must do and something that would be beyond the call of duty. Hence I believe that the shared character of our responsibility in this kind of case does not, in any fundamental way, affect the dilemma outlined in the last section. However, depending on the particular position we take on collective responsibility, we may be subject to *additional* perplexities of non-equivalence arising from the numbers of persons with whom we share responsibility.

11. Triviality and Indifference

Before introducing another principle of general obligation, we must digress briefly to consider how a variety of substantive positions deal with the problem of triviality. In subsequent sections I will argue that approaches to the problem of triviality that work well at the small scale break down at the large scale for a variety of familiar moral positions. This is no minor matter, for it leads to a pervasive moralization of virtually every trivial aspect of everyday life. As a result, the zone of indifference is overwhelmed, and an important pattern of breakdown in the basic structure of individual morality results.

Moral positions vary considerably in the degree to which they take account of the *consequences* of an action in determining moral evaluations. As noted in section 9, some positions are *strictly consequentialist*, i.e., they require that we do whatever we can to bring about better states of the world and that we avoid doing whatever we can to bring about worse states of the world. Such a strictly consequentialist position will routinely violate the assumptions in our basic structure. For if I must do *whatever* will bring about a better state of the world (or avoid a worse one) then I must do so *regardless* of the amount of risk or sacrifice to me—so long as those states of the world, impartially considered, are indeed better or worse in the way supposed. If I could save ten others by sacrificing my life, then so long as the world would indeed be better off after such an action, I am required to be heroic in this way—on the *strict* consequentialist view. A strictly consequentialist position leaves no room for the cutoff for heroism.

Similarly, strict consequentialism leaves no room for a robust sphere of indifference. For so long as states of the world are better or worse, they yield moral requirements for actions that are causally connected to them—regardless of how much, or how little, better or worse they are. Every tiny effect and every tiny increment of risk could determine an action to be right or wrong. As we shall see below, without some cutoff for triviality, consequentialist positions end up violating the robust sphere of indifference. Such a cutoff, however, would be incompatible with the *strictly* consequentialist position, for by ignoring actions producing sufficiently tiny effects, such a cutoff neglects actions that can, infinitesimally, make the world better or worse.

But as noted in section 9, consequentialism need not be so demanding as this "strict" position. We also defined a "weak" position, which is I believe the form that most familiar versions of the doctrine take. According to the weaker doctrine, *if* we are morally required to do (or not to do) an action *X*, it can only be because a better or worse state of the world would result.[1] But some alterations in states of the world, according to this version, need not support moral requirements. For example, when sufficient sacrifice is demanded, no moral requirement need follow, as specified in our cutoff for

---

1. This claim could be formulated in terms of either *actual* or reasonably *expectable* consequences. While this distinction is crucial for some purposes, varieties of consequentialism are compatible with either. Some writers, following Sidgwick's distinction between the utility of an action and the utility of the praise of it, have wished to distinguish the question of whether an agent would be blameworthy (in terms of probable consequences) from whether he would be wrong (in terms of actual consequences). See for example J. J. C. Smart, "Extreme and Restricted Utilitarianism," in Michael D. Bayles, ed., *Contemporary Utilitarianism* (New York: Doubleday, 1968), pp. 99–116, and Smart's discussion of "rational" and "right" actions in "An Outline of a System of Utilitarian Ethics," in Smart and Williams, *Utilitarianism*, pp. 1–74, especially p. 47.

heroism. And when only trivial changes in states of the world would result, no moral requirements need follow, as specified by an assumption we shall define here as the cutoff for triviality. Let us specify this assumption more precisely as follows:

> CUTOFF FOR TRIVIALITY: *Actions with sufficiently insignificant effects (and which raise no other moral issues)*[2] *must be classified as morally indifferent even though effects of the same kind would justify classification of those acts as morally required if those effects were greater in magnitude.*

Let me add that although I believe this assumption to be as noncontroversial as those defined in part I, no essential part of my argument depends on it. In the sections that follow, patterns of breakdown in the basic structure arise under realistic conditions at the large scale—whether or not this assumption is applied. The cases I will discuss clearly violate the robust-sphere-of-indifference assumption. In addition, however, I believe that they should also be interpreted as cases of non-equivalence violating the unique classification assumption. I believe that this interpretation captures the perplexity that many of us will feel when such trivial efforts are regarded as raising moral questions. However, the basic thesis of this book does not depend on this additional claim. And any reader who finds this assumption more controversial should not conclude that the central argument depends on it.

The cutoff for triviality is not a part of the basic structure

---

2. By "other moral issues" I mean issues entirely apart from any consideration of consequences. In other words, some moral positions, perhaps of a deontological variety, for which consequences still have minimal relevance in the sense defined here, may provide some basis for classification of an act as required even when its consequences are trivial (e.g., it may be wrong to break a promise even when its effects are secret and trivial). I mean for this cutoff to apply for cases when such other considerations do *not* apply. Under those circumstances, there are grounds for being troubled when an act is placed in the morally required category—even though its consequences are trivial.

of individual morality defined in part I. It is, however, an assumption that would permit some consequentialist positions (of the weaker variety) to conform to the basic structure by permitting the zone of indifference to be "robust." Without such a cutoff, a host of tiny consequences would yield an overwhelming variety of moral requirements. It is worth emphasizing, however, that the range of positions employing such a cutoff is much broader than the consequentialist family. A moral position need not be even *weakly* consequentialist in order to require such an assumption to avoid moralizing trivial issues. Consequences may have a kind of *minimal relevance* if substantial effects of certain kinds (e.g., harm to others) are regarded as sufficient to take an action out of the zone of indifference. Kantian and absolute moral positions and a variety of other "nonconsequentialist" theories may consistently accept a "minimal relevance" for consequences in this sense. And if they do, a cutoff for triviality would serve to insulate such a position from pervasively moralizing every minor aspect of everyday life.

Charles Fried, for example, endorses such a cutoff explicitly in his defense of an "absolute" prohibition on harming innocent persons. He explains that:

> even absolute notions recognize a concept of triviality. There does indeed seem to be something absurd about wheeling out the heavy moral artillery to deal with pinching. A prohibition may be categorical, but the boundaries of that concept may be susceptible of judgments of degree, at least to the extent that one must recognize the trivial and the absurd.[3]

Richards deals with the same problem by defining his principles so that they only come into play when the morally relevant effects are substantial. One is only obligated to provide mutual aid when it is a matter of avoiding "*great* pain,

---

3. Fried, *Right and Wrong*, p. 31.

injury or even death"; one is only obligated to consider another's interests when it is a matter of "*substantially* advancing" his interests; one is only obligated to intervene paternalistically if it is a matter of "substantially" frustrating the person's interests.[4] Less "great" or "substantial" effects of the same kind are insufficient to engage these principles. They are insufficient in magnitude to define moral duties.

Returning to (weakly) consequentialist theories, Urmson explicitly incorporates such a cutoff for triviality in his version of utilitarianism. Sufficiently trivial effects of a morally relevant kind must be classified as indifferent. Otherwise

> a man who, *ceretis paribus*, chooses the inferior of two musical comedies for an evening's entertainment has done a moral wrong, and this is preposterous.

In attempting to defend the utilitarianism of Mill, Urmson adds:

> If this were in fact the view of Mill, he would indeed be fit for little more than the halting eristic of philosophical infants.

Urmson's solution is a formulation of rule utilitarianism that explicitly incorporates such a cutoff for morally trivial effects. Actions come to be classified as right or wrong in accord with moral rules, and

> Moral rules can be justified only in regard to matters in which the general welfare is *more than negligibly* affected.[5]

Once again, actual effects of a morally relevant kind cannot lead to the classification of an act as right or wrong if those effects are "negligible." Small effects, such as the differences

---

4. Richards, *Theory of Reasons*, pp. 187, 190, 192.

5. J. O. Urmson, "The Interpretation of the Moral Philosophy of J. S. Mill," in Bayles, ed., *Contemporary Utilitarianism*, pp. 13–24. The quotations are from pages 16 and 17.

in utility of two musical comedies, are below the threshold of moral seriousness.

Glover has formulated an interesting objection to this assumption. Because the issue of triviality will be important to us later, his challenge to my approach warrants a digression. Consider his example:

> Suppose a village contains 100 unarmed tribesmen eating their lunch. 100 hungry armed bandits descend on the village and each bandit at gunpoint takes one tribesman's lunch and eats it. The bandits go off, each having done a discriminable amount of harm to a single tribesman.

However, the bandits, troubled by the harm they have done, hit upon a new strategy for their raid the following week. Each tribesman's lunch consists of one hundred baked beans:

> Instead of each bandit eating a single plateful as last week, each takes one bean from each plate. They leave after eating all the beans, pleased to have done no harm as each has done no more than sub-threshold harm to each person.[6]

This case involves what Glover calls a "discrimination threshold"—"where a single person's act will push a situation slightly further in a certain direction, but where his contribution, although real, may be too small to be detected when its effects are spread through the community."[7]

Glover's argument is that we should not count small contributions to a discrimination threshold as if they were zero. For then we would have to conclude, he says, that the bandits each did no harm in the second case (although they obviously did harm in the first). The difficulty, of course, is that the end

---

6. Jonathan Glover, "It Makes No Difference Whether or Not I Do It," *The Aristotelian Society,* Supplementary Volume 49 (1975): 171–90. The quotations are from pp. 174 and 175.

7. Ibid., p. 173.

results of the two cases are the same—each bandit gets one hundred baked beans and each tribesman loses his lunch.

Glover's solution is what he calls the "Principle of Divisibility" for such cases. This principle would count every causal contribution to a "detectable harm" as a divisible part of the harm—no matter how small the fraction. Hence "where a hundred acts like mine are necessary to cause a detectable difference I have caused 1/100th of the detectable harm."[8]

This assumption, in ruling out a threshold, would assign each bandit responsibility for a hundredth of the loss of each tribesman's lunch. None of these harms, as Glover says, are then counted as "zero" and the apparent paradox is avoided by this proposal. Each bandit *does* do harm to each tribesman and those harms add up to a noticeable total, namely, the loss of his lunch.

Now there is a sense in which we could accept Glover's principle of divisibility and, nevertheless, retain a cutoff for triviality. For we must distinguish two issues: (1) the *causal* attribution of responsibility for effects and (2) the moral classification of actions (as indifferent, required or supererogatory) that produce those effects.

We could accept Glover's principle of divisibility as a claim concerning the first issue. It would then be relevant—but not, by itself, decisive—on the second issue. We would still be free, to invoke a cutoff for triviality in our determinations that some actions had effects which were too insignificant to support classifications within the required category (that we were obligated to perform them, or not to perform them).

Let us, therefore, distinguish two proposals:

a. Glover's principle of divisibility interpreted as both a causal and a moral thesis.
b. Glover's principle of divisibility interpreted only as a

---

8. Ibid., p. 174.

causal thesis with the moral classification of actions conditioned by our proposed cutoff for triviality.

Glover's own proposal appears to be a and the point of the bandits example seems to be that proposals such as b lead to inappropriate results when applied to it. I will argue, however, that this is not the case.

Let us assume, with Glover, that one bean is "sub-threshold" and that one hundred beans is an amount far above the threshold. Glover's argument is that each bandit can leave the scene having done "no harm" because "each has done no more than sub-threshold harm to each person." Counting each harm as "zero," it obviously follows that one hundred times zero is also zero. Hence, denial of the principle of divisibility—through the assertion of such a threshold—appears to lead us to the conclusion that we cannot attribute responsibility to each bandit for a total of one lunch lost (one hundred beans).

However, proposal b would not have this implication. For by Glover's own principle of divisibility we can attribute responsibility to each bandit for stealing one lunch. For one hundred bandits together steal one hundred lunches through a series of identical actions. By the princple of divisibility they must equally divide responsibility for this collective result. One-hundredth responsibility for one hundred lunches yields responsibility for one lunch (i.e., one hundred baked beans). Since one lunch was assumed to be above the threshold, responsibility for one lunch is sufficient for us to judge each bandit wrong. Hence we can reach the same conclusion about the second week's raid as we obviously reached about the first week's: each bandit has responsibility for stealing one lunch.

The difference between the two proposals is that b would not permit us morally to condemn a bandit who stole so few baked beans that it added up to an amount below the threshold. We could still attribute *causal* responsibility for their disappearance to the bandit. However, if the total amount was sufficiently trivial, it would not be enough to support our classifying the action as right or wrong.

Glover's mistake appears to be the covert assumption of a different kind of divisibility—namely, that a person cannot harm a group unless he harms some identifiable individual within it. This seems to be the basis for his inference that each bandit can leave the scene having done "no harm"—"as each has done no more than sub-threshold harm to *each* person." Corresponding to each bandit, there is no identifiable individual whom he has harmed (to any morally significant extent). But it does not follow that he has not, in total, done a significant amount of harm. Hence, even by the principle of divisibility, a one hundredth share of the total harm done to the group of one hundred persons is an amount of harm above the threshold—one lunch lost.

A second point to be made about Glover's principle of divisibility—applied as a moral (as well as a causal) thesis—is that consistent application of this principle would very quickly erode away the zone of moral indifference. Consider, for example, the moral problems my wife and I would face in planning the dinner party mentioned earlier. Can we serve beef? We are then contributing infinitesimally to the world food crisis, because we are encouraging, in a tiny way, a practice that leads to wasting much of the world's food resources. By the principle of divisibility, it does not matter how small the effects are, so long as they are *some* minute fraction of effects that are, in aggregate, significant.

Consider the effects on our guests. Like other typical adult Americans, there is a significant risk that each of them may die of heart disease or cancer. Assuming that these risks are morally significant, implications for our dinner party follow from the principle of divisibility. For if we serve high-cholesterol foods or fattening deserts, we increase, in a tiny way, their risk of heart disease; similarly, if we serve foods with various chemical additives or artificial sweeteners, we increase, in a tiny way, their risk of cancer. By the principle of divisibility, these tiny increments—no matter how small—must count for the moral determination of our actions as right or wrong. It should be clear that by this principle we face a host of unexpected moral questions. The pervasive moralization of the zone of indifference would quickly follow from such a position.

By our *b* alternative, however, these tiny effects and tiny increments of risk can be treated as falling below the threshold of moral significance. We can accept Glover's causal thesis while avoiding the pervasive moralization of every trivial aspect of everyday life and the attendant breakdown in the robust zone of indifference.

12. What If Everyone Did That?

Let me now introduce another principle of general obligation, the generalization argument. My argument will be that breakdowns in the basic structure arise for this principle in two ways. First, if positions incorporate the cutoff for triviality introduced in the last section, then non-equivalence problems result. Second, overload problems inevitably arise at the large scale, violating both the robust sphere of indifference and the cutoff for heroism.

Even those who have argued against the principle of generalization have usually agreed that it is one of our most commonly invoked moral conceptions. For example, C. D. Broad, who wrote a classic critique, regarded his target as the principle that is "perhaps more explicitly used in the reasonings of daily life than any other."[1]

David Lyons offers a good specimen of the way this principle is commonly employed:

> "Oh Look!" she said, pointing off to the right. "The apples are ripe in that orchard. Let's stop and pick some."
>
> "No...." He drove on, more slowly. "I don't think we should. Suppose everyone did that!"
>
> "Don't be silly—not everyone will. And the few we'd take wouldn't be missed."
>
> "But that's beside the point. If we can do it then so can anyone else. And if everyone did the same...."

---

1. C. D. Broad, "On the Function of False Hypothesis in Ethics,"

Here the *hypothetical* consequences of everyone's doing the same are invoked as a sufficient condition for classifying the action as wrong. The fact that everyone, in fact, will not do it is "beside the point."[2]

Kant, of course, regarded a closely related argument as the fundamental principle of morality. Consider this formulation of the Categorical Imperative:

Act only on that maxim through which you can at the same time will that it should become a universal law.[3]

This fundamental principle produces a two-part test that Kant would have us apply to the maxims of our actions. First, there are cases where, if we attempt to will the maxim of an action universally, we contradict ourselves. Second, there are cases where a maxim could be applied universally without self-contradiction, but we cannot, despite that fact, *will* that it should hold as a universal law.

Kant offers as an example of the first kind of case a man who borrows money without intending to pay it back. He must ask himself, "How would things stand if my maxim became a universal law?" Kant concludes that such a maxim "must necessarily contradict itself" as a universal law:

For the universality of a law that every one believing himself to be in need can make any promise he pleases with the intention not to keep it would make promising, itself, impossible, since no one would believe he was being promised anything, but would laugh at utterances of this kind as empty shams.[4]

International Journal of Ethics 26 (1915–16): 377–97. The quotation is from page 377.

2. Lyons, *Forms and Limits of Utilitarianism,* p. 2.

3. Kant, *Groundwork of the Metaphysic of Morals,* p. 88 (p. 51, 2nd ed.). This is the most famous of five formulas for the categorical imperative. For a discussion of the different versions, see H. J. Paton, *The Categorical Imperative* (Philadelphia: University of Pennsylvania Press, 1971), pp. 129–98.

4. Kant, *Groundwork,* p. 90. (p. 55, 2nd ed.).

Here the self-contradiction depends upon the results Kant envisages of a *universal* practice of making such promises— that promising would itself become impossible under such conditions.

An example of the second part of the test, according to Kant, is the man who neglects his talents for idleness and enjoyment. When he applies the categorical imperative:

> He then sees that a system of nature could indeed always subsist under such a universal law, although (like the South Sea Islanders) every man should let his talents rust and should be bent on devoting his life solely to idleness, indulgence, procreation and, in a word, to enjoyment.[5]

However, even though this maxim can be consistently applied as a universal law, a rational being, Kant believes, "cannot possibly *will* that this should become a universal law of nature."

> For as a rational being he necessarily wills that all his powers should be developed, since they serve him, and are given him, for all sorts of possible ends.[6]

Whatever we think of the ambiguities of this second version of the test, it should be clear that in both versions Kant is concerned with the moral significance of the "universal" (or general) performance of the action being evaluated. Consequences—such as the hypothetical breakdown of the practice of promising and the hypothetical creation of a world of idleness like that of the South Sea Islanders—are clearly a part of this evaluation. How the moral "will" is supposed to autonomously approve of some of these universal laws, but not others, remains, admittedly, a bit mysterious. For this reason we will not investigate the properties of Kant's own precise version of the generalization argument, but rather, of modern

5. Ibid.
6. Ibid.

versions which are immune from these ambiguities and which incorporate certain recognizably Kantian elements.

One example of such a modern, Kantian version of the generalization argument is Marcus Singer's principle:

> If everyone were to do X, the consequences would be disastrous (or undesirable): therefore no one ought to do X.[7]

Harrod and Ewing both have similarly interpreted the moral significance of the *consequences* of everybody doing the same as the "Kantian" principle of generalization.[8] It is in this form that the argument is commonly employed. As Ewing notes:

> Kant thought that what made a principle wrong was that its universalization would involve some inconsistency, either a sheer logical contradiction, or an inconsistency with what we could not help willing.... But as generally used the argument is not that we could not conceive or at least not consistently will the universalization of a principle, but simply that its universalization would lead to bad consequences.[9]

What we will treat here as the "Kantian" principle of generalization would have us envision the hypothetical consequences that would result from a general pattern of others doing the same. This principle requires us to ask, "What if everyone did that?" We are then to evaluate the act based on the hypothetical consequences that would result.

These modern versions are recognizably Kantian because—unlike other versions of generalization—their impli-

7. Marcus George Singer, *Generalization in Ethics* (New York: Atheneum, 1971), p. 61.

8. R. F. Harrod, "Utilitarianism Revised," *Mind* 45 (1936): 137–56; A. C. Ewing, "What Would Happen If Everybody Acted Like Me?" *Philosophy* 28 (1953): 16–29.

9. Ewing, "What Would Happen?" p. 16. For an identification of this form of hypothetical "rule utilitarianism" with Kant, see J.J.C. Smart, "An Outline of a System of Utilitarian Ethics," pp. 9–11.

cations do not vary depending on the actual behavior of others. For the Kantian, my duty to do X (or not to do X) does not vary depending on whether others are also actually doing their duty. As we shall see, other versions of generalization differ markedly on this point.

For example, the generalization argument is also susceptible to a strictly *utilitarian* interpretation, which has been systematically examined by David Lyons. In this form we must carefully determine *all* of the actual effects of a given action. The generalization test then bids us to envision the consequences of everyone doing the same—where the "same" is strictly limited to those actions that would have precisely the same consequences as the act actually had. Lyons argues that, in this strictly utilitarian form, the generalization test is equivalent to simple utilitarianism (the doctrine that an act should be morally evaluated by its own actual consequences). According to Lyons, the two criteria, the generalization argument and simple utilitarianism, can never lead to differing moral conclusions—provided that the generalization argument is applied in a strictly utilitarian fashion.[10]

Later, I shall argue that even the strictly utilitarian version leads to results that depart from simple utilitarianism at the large scale. This result dramatizes one of the ways in which individual morality becomes especially problematical when large numbers are involved.

For the moment, however, we need only note that the generalization argument is a venerable principle of general obligation which, like the principle of minimal altruism discussed earlier, has both Kantian and utilitarian proponents. It has been employed, in other words, by theorists who otherwise disagree in fundamental respects. Let us formulate this assumption more precisely:

---

10. Lyons, *Forms and Limits* chapter 3.

THE RELEVANCE OF GENERALIZATION: *A sufficient condition for an act's being morally required (positively or negatively) is the moral significance of the general performance of the "same" action.*[11]

As we will later explore in some detail, the Kantian and utilitarian versions of generalization depend on radically different interpretations of "the same." Because the actual effects of a given act may depend, crucially, on the causal context provided by the behavior of others, the utilitarian version must take account of the actual behavior of others in determining the precise description of the act to be generalized. If my not voting has insignificant effects *because* it is an isolated act (of not voting), then the utilitarian generalization of *that* act can only range over a number of other acts that are equally inconsequential—because they are also isolated. Kantian generalization, by contrast, would bar this calculation that the act turns out to be insignificant because of the actual behavior of others. The Kantian generalization of the act of not voting would envision *everyone* in the society (who could vote) not voting. The interpretation of "the same" act is not restricted by descriptions of the act that include a description of the (causally relevent) actual behavior of others.

Both Kantian and utilitarian generalization principles are "dependent" (rather than "independent") in the sense defined earlier. The former version is dependent upon hypothetical assumptions about the (morally appropriate) behavior of others, and the latter, on a determination of the actual behavior of others. I shall not take a position on the question of which version of generalization is more adequate. I intend, rather, to argue that they share a common problem. They both lead to breakdowns in the basic structure of individual morality at the large scale.

---

11. I use the phrase "moral significance" to cover the straightforward case of "significant consequences" and to cover, as well, the more mysterious determinations of the Kantian moral will.

13. The Moral Microscope

There is a rich literature on moral generalization that has focused on the question, Does it matter whether we evaluate an act by its consequences, considered by themselves, or by the consequences that would result if everybody did the "same"? Until recently, the consensus clearly held that it *did* matter which of these two criteria were applied to a given act. These two criteria would, in other words, sometimes support substantively different conclusions when applied to the same act considered in the same way. For in a wide variety of cases, an individual act would apparently have trivial or insignificant consequences even though the same act, if generalized over a large number of similar performances, would be morally significant. Which of these two criteria were more adequate then became a subject of hot contention.

However, David Lyons, in an original and important book, has argued systematically that the difference between these two criteria is illusory.[1] If an act has good, bad, or indifferent generalized consequences, then it must also have consequences of the same moral quality when considered by itself. Hence, the kind of case that will principally concern us—indifferent individual consequences corresponding to good or bad generalized consequences—cannot arise.

So long as we adhere to the cutoff for triviality, Lyons's claim must be mistaken for a kind of case that can arise at the large scale. Although his thesis is correct at the small scale,

---

1. Lyons, *Forms and Limits of Utilitarianism.*

there is a kind of case that arises uniquely at the large scale which offers a genuine exception to it. This kind of case, furthermore, corresponds to some of the examples that have been regarded as problematical throughout the literature on moral generalization. However, their relation to scale has not been systematically explored. Only at the large scale can an act have consequences so trivial that it should be classified as morally indifferent, even though the same act when generalized would be morally significant.

On the other hand, were we to preserve Lyons's thesis by refusing to admit the cutoff for triviality, then every trivial effect would be sufficient to determine moral requirements. The zone of indifference would collapse under the weight of the host of moral demands determined by every tiny consequence. In the following discussion I will assume the cutoff for triviality in order to keep the zone of indifference intact. That way, we will be able to evaluate the changing implications of moral generalization with increasing numbers. Later, I will return to the cutoff for triviality to consider further the kind of position that results if this assumption is rejected.

With the cutoff for triviality in place, the problem forestalled at the small scale arises with increasing numbers. It can be posed as a kind of dilemma. If we were consistently to apply the generalization principle as a guide to conduct at the large scale, a pervasive moralization of everyday life would result. For however trivial the individual consequences of an act, when it is generalized over a large enough number of other similar acts its consequences will routinely be enlarged to a level of moral significance. As a result, the zone of indifference would collapse in the face of the generalization argument applied consistently at the large scale. Nearly everything would become a moral question and that discretionary space where we can, morally speaking, do as we please would disappear. The basic structure would collapse because the zone of indifference could no longer be robust.

On the other hand, if we were to reject the generalization

argument we would find ourselves without the one principle that has been most potently applied against the free-rider and the defaulter. Why should I vote if my individual vote cannot be expected to make a difference anyway? Why should I pay my taxes (if I could somehow get away without doing so), since what I pay will, by itself, make no difference? Why should I keep my thermostat adjusted to save energy, since the amount I can save must be trivial in its total effects? Questions such as these have traditionally found a powerful response in the generalization argument. If everyone failed to vote, the institutions of democracy would collapse; if everyone failed to pay taxes, the government would go bankrupt; if everyone failed to conserve energy, national policy would be seriously affected.

Hence we are faced with a dilemma: On the one hand, if we were to adhere, consistently, to the implications of the generalization argument at the large scale, a pervasive moralization of everyday life would result. Nearly every action or inaction would give rise to a moral question. On the other hand, if we were to relinquish the generalization argument at the large scale, we would lose what has traditionally been the most potent argument against the free-rider, the defaulter, the tax-evader, the nonvoter—namely, the argument, What if everyone did that?

My purpose in this section is not to resolve this dilemma but, rather, to formulate it systematically. My claim is that it can arise only at the large scale: For only when the numbers are large enough will the generalization argument routinely magnify the trivial to a level of moral significance. This pervasive magnification of trivial consequences can be viewed as a threefold breakdown in the basic structure of individual morality. Most obviously, it implies a collapse in the robust zone of indifference. Secondly, if the cutoff for triviality is accepted, then acts are classified as both indifferent and required so that such cases violate the unique classification assumption. Thirdly, once the zone of indifference has been systematically supplanted by moral requirements, we would find ourselves obligated to give up the entire way of life we take for granted. As noted earlier, this can plausibly be viewed as too demanding a requirement, more appropriate for saints or heroes than for ordinary persons.

Let us begin by examining the cases that have traditionally been thought to be problematical in the literature on moral generalization. Then let us turn to Lyons's argument, which attempts to prove that these problematical results are illusory. A critique of Lyons's argument will enable me to make my point about the problematical character of generalization arguments at the large scale. We will then see that this critique applies, as well, to Kantian versions. The same patterns of breakdown in the basic structure arise for both versions of the argument.

Some of the special implications of moral generalization at the large scale were noted by C. D. Broad more than sixty years ago. He remarked that the principle of generalization could serve as "a moral microscope":

> The result of one man's action may be very small, and it may be impossible for him to see by contemplating it alone whether it be good, bad, or indifferent. But he may be able to see that a great number of such actions would produce a result of the same kind as a single one but of much greater magnitude, and that this result would be unmistakably good or bad.[2]

Broad offers this example:

> I walk through a field and pluck an ear of corn. Is this right, wrong or indifferent? If I now say: Suppose a million people walked through and each plucked an ear, the results would be very bad.[3]

---

2. Broad, "On the Function of False Hypothesis in Ethics," p. 382.
3. Ibid., p. 383.

Even though this use of the principle is exceedingly common, Broad argues that it is "most precarious." For "my walking through may have done no damage whatever, but it would be physically impossible for a million people to walk through without doing grave damage." Even when we consider the psychological (as well as economic) effects on the owner from his ears of corn being plucked, "it seems perfectly possible that no one's state of mind is in the least better or worse for the plucking of one ear and yet it may be very much the worse for the plucking of a million."[4] The difficulty is, that the "moral microscope" may lead us to a judgment quite different from any we might reach about the consequences of the act considered by itself. The microscope, if sufficiently powerful, magnifies not only the plucking of an ear of corn but also the consequences of a host of other minor acts such as walking through the field. Surely, whatever we think of the latter act, its consequences considered alone must be trivial. For purposes of moral evaluation, walking through the field must be considered an act that does "no damage whatever." Yet, a large enough number of others doing the same would surely ruin the field.

Some twenty years later, R. F. Harrod identified some related problematical cases. He argued that the "Kantian principle" of generalization and the "crude utilitarian principle" of individual consequences could diverge. Considering the problem of lying in utilitarian terms, he concluded:

it may well happen that the loss of confidence due to a million lies uttered within certain limits of time and space is much more than a million times as great as the loss due to any one in particular. Consequently, even if on each and every occasion taken separately it can be shown that there is a gain of advantage...yet in the sum of all cases the disadvantage due to the aggregate loss of

4. Ibid.

confidence might be far greater than the sum of pain caused by truth-telling.

This kind of example led Harrod to the conclusion that:

> there are certain acts which when performed on n similar occasions have consequences more than n times as great as those resulting from one performance.[5]

As we shall later see, Harrod misidentified the class of problematical cases. As Lyons argues, Harrod's description of these cases neglects a crucial factor, threshold effects. However, I will later argue that cases which are similar to Harrod's example *can* yield divergent results even when threshold effects are accounted for as Lyons proposes. Without realizing it, Harrod posed cases that were complicated by two distinct factors: threshold effects and social scale. While Lyons is correct to criticize Harrod's neglect of the former, we will find reason to criticize Lyons's neglect of the latter.

About thirty years after Harrod's article, Jonathan Harrison offered some further cases which, like Harrod's, involved these twin factors of threshold effects and social scale. Harrison regarded them as problematical because our duties in such cases could not be accounted for by simple utilitarianism:

> There are some actions which we think we have a duty to do, although they themselves produce no good consequences, because such actions would produce good consequences if they were generally practiced. There are some actions which we think we have a duty to refrain from doing, even though they themselves produce no harmful consequences, because such actions would produce harmful consequences if performance of them became the general rule.

---

5. Harrod, "Utilitarianism Revised," p. 148.

Harrison offered two examples. First, I may regard myself as having a duty to vote "although I do not think that the addition of my vote...is going to make any difference to the result of the election." And second, I may regard myself as required to avoid walking "on the grass of a well-kept park lawn," even though I know that my walking on the grass will not, by itself, do any significant damage whatsoever. Even if no one was aware that I had walked on the grass or that I had failed to vote, I might regard myself as obligated in these cases because of the consequences that *would* result from others generally not voting, or others generally walking on the grass.[6]

A. C. Ewing also identified some cases of utilitarian generalization that were "peculiar and puzzling"—cases that, like those offered by Broad, Harrod, and Harrison, depend implicitly on social scale for their problematical character. For example, even though an individual taxpayer might regard his own payments as merely "a drop in the bucket" that could not make any appreciable difference to government expenditures or services, the generalized consequences (assuming each individual could get away with it) of everybody doing the "same" would be disastrous. Ewing similarly argued that refusing to enlist during the war would have been wrong because of "not just the effects of one man refusing to enlist but the effects that would result if this attitude spread to most people, though in fact there was no reason whatever to anticipate that it would spread to most people."

The way in which the individual and generalized consequences of the "same" act may support differing moral conclusions appears to be even clearer in Ewing's example of a "parliamentary election":

> Except in the extraordinarily rare case where a seat is won by a single vote, which we can dismiss as too extremely

---

6. Jonathan Harrison, "Utilitarianism, Universilization and Our Duty to Be Just," reprinted in Bayles, ed., *Contemporary Utilitarianism*, pp. 25–57. The quotations are from pp. 27–28.

unlikely to be worth considering, one man's vote will make no appreciable difference whatever, yet we should still hold it his duty to vote and vote as intelligently as he could on the ground not of the effects of his particular vote but of the effects which would accrue if it were a general practice not to vote or to vote without reflection.[7]

Here the individual consequences appear clearly negligible, while the generalized consequences, on the other hand, of everyone (presumably all of those eligible to vote) doing the "same" appears to be of obvious significance.

Similar examples of apparent divergence between the individual and the generalized consequences of the "same" act have been noted by other writers. A. K. Stout, in a kind of example also used by Brandt, discussed an individual using extra water or electricity during a "drought" or a "power shortage." Even though the individual consequences may be negligible ["the little drop I need...won't make any difference and no one will know." Or: "just my small electric fire won't count."] Stout points out that: "In all such cases we can be pulled up short by 'But suppose everyone did it.'"[8]

7. Ewing, "What Would Happen?" p. 18. Similar applications of generalization arguments to voting and large-scale political participation can be found in Paul E. Meehl, "The Selfish Voter Paradox and the Thrown-Away Vote Argument," The American Political Science Review 81 (1977): 11–30, and Stanley I. Benn, "The Problematic Rationality of Political Participation," in Laslett and Fishkin, eds., Philosophy, Politics and Society, pp. 291–312. Note the example on page 291.

8. A. K. Stout, "But Suppose Everyone Did the Same," The Australian Journal of Philosophy 32 (1954): 1–29. The quotations are from p. 16.

14. Lyons's Argument

As we have just seen, the literature on moral generalization yields a host of familiar examples where the individual and generalized consequences of the same act appear to support conflicting moral conclusions. Because of an act's trivial individual consequences, it appears to be morally indifferent. But because of its significant generalized consequences, it appears to be morally required. Such apparent cases of nonequivalence are a routine part of everyday life. Because such cases represent an important and familiar pattern of breakdown in our assumptions at the large scale, Lyons's systematic argument that we must be mistaken about them will be considered in detail. My critique of Lyons's argument will then provide a basis for establishing several related patterns of breakdown in the basic structure at the large scale.

Why must I vote if my individual vote, by itself, can be expected to make no difference? But if everyone failed to vote, the results would be disastrous. Why must I not walk in the field and pluck an ear of corn (in Broad's example)? But if everyone did the same, the man's field would be ruined. Why must I not use extra water or electricity when there is a need for conservation? The little bit I use won't make any difference. But if everyone did the same?

Lyons contends that these problematical cases are illusory. We are mistaken if we believe that the individual and generalized consequences of the same act can support such conflicting moral conclusions. Or, at least, this is Lyons's thesis provided that we adopt a utilitarian interpretation of what is meant by the "same act." Later we will see that, regardless of whether we adopt Lyons's utilitarian interpretation or the alternative Kantian version of hypothetical generalization, there is a problematical class of cases which do support conflicting moral conclusions—but only at the large scale. For the moment, however, let us examine Lyons's argument.

He claims that if we "take care to exclude extraneous factors" we will find that the individual and generalized consequences yield "equivalent judgments in all cases," provided that "the generalization is given a purely utilitarian interpretation."[1]

Now by a purely "utilitarian" interpretation Lyons does not mean to imply any restriction on the kinds of consequences that can be taken into account by either the individual or the generalized consequences principle:

> we are not assuming that a utilitarian theory is necessarily hedonistic, for example, (i.e. based upon a pleasure principle) and we need impose no other evaluative restrictions.[2]

Rather, the argument is meant to be "strictly schematic requiring no specification of value criteria."[3] It is for this reason, in fact, that it "purports to be conclusive."[4] All that is required is that:

> When principles are compared, the value criteria employed in conjunction with them must, of course, be (whatever else they are) identical.[5]

Lyons's point, then, is to establish that the difference in "structure" between the two criteria, by itself, makes no difference.[6] This is the claim I shall dispute.

1. Lyons, *Forms and Limits of Utilitarianism*, p. x.
2. Ibid., p. 5.
3. Ibid., p. 6.
4. Ibid., p. xi.
5. Ibid., p. 6.
6. Ibid., p. 5.

Lyons's method is to "hazard an argument on *a priori* grounds"—an argument directed against "the line of reasoning which would lead one quite naturally to suppose that non-equivalence obtains."[7] By "non-equivalence" here he means conflicting moral conclusions resulting from the two criteria: the individual consequences of an act and the generalized consequences of everyone's doing the same. Lyons argues that this conjectured route to "non-equivalence"—via a condition of what he calls "non-linearity" among relevantly similar acts—is incompatible with a thoroughgoing *utilitarian* interpretation of moral generalization.

We can roughly summarize Lyons's general strategy as follows: If actions are "non-linear" then they have unequal effects; and if they have unequal effects then they cannot be relevantly similar; if they are not relevantly similar then they cannot, in other words, constitute cases of the "same" act. Hence, if we take care to generalize acts only over those cases that *are* relevantly similar, we will not include acts with differing (or "non-linear" effects). Hence the notion that non-linear effects result from relevantly similar acts must rest on a confusion.

It is worth mentioning that we will later encounter cases of "non-equivalence" under the precise condition that Lyons believes must guarantee equivalence. In other words, if we accept, for purposes of argument, Lyons's critique of the "non-linear" cases, we can arrive, nevertheless, at cases of "non-equivalence" at the large scale.

The argument for non-equivalence which Lyons refutes is based on the notion that there can be an "irregularity" in the contribution of relevantly similar acts to the total consequences envisioned by a moral generalization. By an "irregularity" Lyons means the kind of relation posited by Harrod when he claimed that there were acts "which when performed on n similar occasions have consequences *more than*

---

7. Ibid., p. 62.

n times as great as those resulting from one performance."
This claim, which Lyons dubs "Harrod's paradox," requires
that acts which have differing consequences be accepted,
nevertheless, as relevantly similar.[8] If, however, acts have differing consequences because of the causal context provided
by the behavior of others, then they are no longer relevantly
similar—precisely because to be relevantly similar they must
have similar effects. Hence Harrod's paradox is incompatible
with a *utilitarian* interpretation of relevant similarity. This
utilitarian interpretation is that acts are relevantly similar
when they have the same effects. If apparently similar acts
have differing effects when performed more frequently, then
they are simply not "relevantly similar" for purposes of moral
generalization.

Acts are relevantly similar when they have identical effects (or make identical contributions to an aggregate effect).
This means that it is easy to state the relation between the individual (or "simple") consequences of an act, considered by
itself, and the generalized consequences of everyone's doing
the "same":

> Let G represent the generalized utility of a given act—the
> value of everyone's doing the same in respect of a given
> description; and let S represent the simple utility. There
> will be n occasions for doing the kind of act in question;
> that is, if everyone who had occasion to do so on each
> such occasion did the sort of act described, that sort of act
> would be performed n times. Linearity then obtains when
> $G = n \times S$; any other relation is non-linear.[9]

There would appear to be an obvious argument for the relationship between linearity and equivalence. If linearity obtains, then how could S and G differ in quality? And if S and G

---

8. Ibid., p. 66.
9. Ibid., p. 65.

do not differ in quality, then how could there be non-equivalence? As Lyons explains:

> non-linearity is a necessary condition of a qualitative dif-ference between G and S; for if G and S have different qualities, then they cannot in any way be proportional, and hence not proportional in this special way.[10]

The argument, in other words, is that G must equal N × S for relevantly similar acts. Hence if G is positive, then S must also be, and if G is negative, then S must also be (since S = G/N). Hence G and S must always have the same moral qual-ity; hence they must always support equivalent moral conclu-sions.

Lyons believes that we arrive at the illusion of non-equivalence by neglecting a "causal factor" of crucial impor-tance—i.e., "threshold" effects. Typically, we may consider the individual act in isolation and, as a result, neglect its pos-sible contribution to the triggering of a threshold. It is by con-sidering the act "in vacuo," in isolation from its possible threshold effects (or other effects that depend upon the causal context provided by the behavior of others), that we may falsely arrive at "non-equivalent" results.

There are two ways this may occur. Case 1 concerns an act that is not performed in the context of a general pattern of others doing the same. However, if this kind of act were, in fact, performed by enough others it would trigger a threshold. Perhaps a relatively isolated act of not voting, or of walking on the grass, or of defaulting on one's taxes, or of taking more than one's share of water or electricity (when these are rationed) will do no harm. But if enough others were to do the same, morally significant consequences would result. In such cases we are led to the illusion of non-equivalence, Lyons argues, because we correctly estimate the individual conse-quences of the isolated act to be negligible (and hence indif-

---

10. Ibid.

ferent) but we incorrectly estimate the generalized consequences. For we wrongly generalize the act over enough
others to include the hypothetical threshold effects. These
threshold effects render the generalized consequences significant even though the individual consequences of the isolated act were rightly estimated to be insignificant. Since the
generalization should only range over acts that are relevantly
similar in that they have the same actual effects, we are mistaken to include threshold-triggering acts in the generalization when the individual act did not actually have effects of
that kind.

Hence if an individual act of not voting, or of walking on
the grass, or of taking more than one's share of a rationed
commodity is sufficiently *isolated* that it has no significant effects, then the generalization of that act can only range over a
number of others who could do the same. Here, by the "same"
we must mean "not voting when so few others do the same
that the act is inconsequential" or "walking on the grass when
so few others do the same that the act is inconsequential."

In other words, the act must be described "completely."
By this, Lyons means that all of the factors relevant to the act's
actual effects must be included in the description. It is this
complete description of the act that then determines how
many could actually do the "same." In these cases, when an
act has inconsequential effects *because* it is isolated, its
(utilitarian) generalization can only range over a number of
other acts sufficiently small that they each have effects identical to the original isolated act. Lyons argues that it is by neglecting the complete description—permitting the generalization to include threshold-related effects when none were
present in the original act—that we can be led to conclude
that the generalized consequences are significant even
though the individual, isolated act is clearly insignificant.

The case of apparent non-equivalence just discussed involves an act that is actually isolated from a (threshold-

related) general pattern. It is the act's isolation which renders its actual consequences insignificant. Consider now a second kind of case concerning acts that are *not* isolated; they are, rather, performed in the context of a (threshold-related) general pattern of others doing the same. Suppose that I walk on the lawn while enough others are doing the same so that together we ruin it. Or suppose that there is a mass abstention at the polls and my not voting contributes to whatever significant effects actually result (whether negative or positive). In these cases the act is performed within, rather than outside of, a general pattern of others doing the same.

However, unless we are careful, it is also easy to neglect the threshold effects in this kind of case. For if we correctly include the threshold effects of the actual pattern in the generalized consequences (the effects of *everyone* actually walking on the grass or not voting) we will conclude that the latter are significant. However, once more, if we view the individual act in isolation ("in vacuo") we may not include those same threshold effects in our estimation of the act's individual consequences. And unless this contribution to the threshold is reckoned in, the individual act will appear trivial.

So the difficulty in this second case is that even if we correctly assess the threshold effects of the generalized consequences, we may arrive at non-equivalence by failing to count them in the individual consequences. By contrast, the difficulty in the first case was that even if we correctly assess the individual consequences, we may arrive at non-equivalence by wrongly counting threshold effects in the generalized consequences. In both cases the disparity is the result (rightly or wrongly) of counting threshold effects in the generalized consequences while not counting them when we consider the act by itself. It is on this mistake that the illusion of an "irregularity" or "non-linearity" among relevantly similar acts rests.

Lyons's argument is that when the description of an act is "complete," *i.e.*, when it includes, in addition to all other effects, a specification of whether or not the act is performed in the context of a pattern sufficiently general for it to contribute to a threshold, then its generalization is restricted to that class of acts which may, in the same way, succeed or fail in contributing to the threshold. "Thus," as Lyons explains:

> ordinarily a few individuals can cross the lawn without doing appreciable damage; a few supporters can abstain without affecting their candidate's chances; a few lies can be told, a few promises broken, a few goods sold on the black market; a few citizens can evade their taxes and military service or exploit rationing restrictions—to take but a few of the commonest examples of utilitarian generalization—without undesirable effects on the whole, provided that most others do not do such things.[11]

---

11. Ibid., p. 71.

15. Thresholds and Triviality

Let us examine Lyons's argument more carefully. How does reckoning in the threshold effects guarantee that equivalence will always be restored? First, more needs to be said about how the effects of an act may vary depending on how many others do the "same." Consider Lyons's explanation of "thresholds":

> For many kinds of acts there are *thresholds* [emphasis in original] which must be passed before effects of certain kinds or of certain magnitudes can be produced. For many kinds of acts, in other words, *the curves describing the relation between total effect and the number of performances are irregular or at least not straight lines.* [emphasis added][1]

For example, we might imagine a well-defined threshold pictured in figure 1. The addition of the mth performance of an action triggers a precipitous change in total effect, pictured on the vertical axis. The mth act may represent the proverbial "straw" that proves too much for the camel, or the vote that decides the election, or the added electrical appliance that blows the fuse.

Or we might imagine an act whose effects are strictly "linear" throughout. As in figure 2, no matter how often the act is performed, each additional performance contributes the same precise amount to the total effect. Linear intervals can,

---

1. Lyons, *Forms and Limits of Utilitarianism,* p. 72.

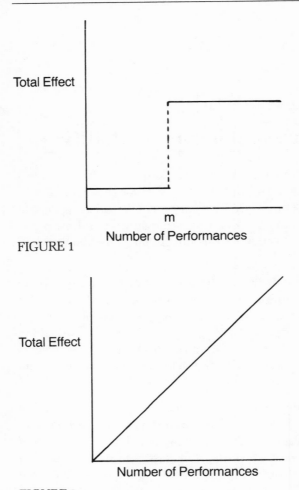

Total Effect

m

Number of Performances

FIGURE 1

Total Effect

Number of Performances

FIGURE 2

in other words, be pictured as straight lines. Each drop in the bucket adds precisely the same amount to the total; or perhaps each dollar to famine relief pays for the same amount of food (at least over some interval).

Or, as Lyons notes, the curves may be more "irregular." Imagine, for example, a public demonstration. If the numbers who show up are very small, each additional participant may add little to the collective effect. As the numbers build, each may begin to add more than the last as the demonstration becomes more clearly a success. By contrast, when the numbers become great enough, additional participants may decline in value (in their contributions to the collective effect of the demonstration). It may be almost indistinguishable whether 5,000 or 5,001 persons show up on the steps of City Hall. Yet if I had been one of only 30 people, my presence would have been much more noticeable. We may be able to roughly identify these variations in an individual's effect without there being any well-defined threshold. The point is that the effects of an individual's act may vary markedly with how many others are doing the same—even though there is no well-defined threshold and even though the effects are not linear. Figure 3 roughly depicts such a situation. In order to know the effects of my participation in the demonstration at City Hall, we have to know how many are doing likewise.

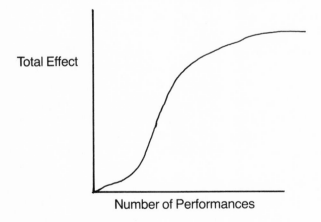

FIGURE 3

Of course, these examples barely touch on the variety of possible patterns of variation. Yet for Lyons's argument, we need do no more than distinguish the linear case (as in figure 2) from all others. For Lyons's strategy is to reduce all of the more complex cases to a sequence of "homogeneous sub-classes" that can be treated as linear in the sense that they are credited with precisely similar effects. After giving due credit for contributions to the triggering of a threshold, we simply divide up those more complex cases into intervals of one or more acts that have precisely similar effects. It is only acts within these intervals that are "relevantly similar" to each other for purposes of moral generalization.

Before generalizing it, we must determine an act's precise actual effects. If the act is linear as in figure 2, this task is simple. If it is nonlinear, then we must determine the effects of the act in the causal context provided by the behavior of others. We must, in other words, determine its horizontal location on a graph such as figure 1 or 3 (or any other non-linear case).

It may be that the homogeneous sub-classes which result are sometimes "unit classes." Lyons explicitly allows for this possibility. It means only that we have asked the question, What if everyone did that? about an act which only *one* person could perform. Suppose, in a legislature, that the number of favorable votes for a measure is well known—and one vote short of the m votes needed for passage. The addition of the mth vote to the already extant coalition is a unique act clearly distinguishable in its effects from the previous m-1 votes. It is known, in this case, which act triggers a threshold (such as that in figure 1). Only one person could actually provide the decisive vote. The generalization of *that* act could only range over a unit class.

By contrast, credit for triggering a threshold will sometimes be distributed over many acts. Consider the case of simultaneous voting by secret ballot—when the votes of others are not known. Lyons argues that since we cannot distinguish the vote which triggers the threshold (the mth vote required to win) we should treal all m votes as equally contributing to the threshold. Each vote can then be credited with

1/m of the collective effect. For example, if the threshold were the one depicted in figure 4, then the new linear class which would be defined can be pictured by the dotted line traced out diagonally to m. For each act would then be assessed an equal share (1/mth) of the collective threshold effect.

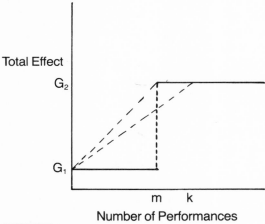

Total Effect

G_2

G_1

m   k

Number of Performances

FIGURE 4

Or, if a number (let us call it k) greater than the threshold is received by the winning candidate, we would not be able to distinguish the surplus votes (those more than the m required for victory). Lyons's proposal is that we credit each vote with 1/k of the collective effect. In that case the new linear class traced out by the second dotted line would be defined.

Voting offers thresholds that are unusually well defined, but the same procedure can be applied to any kind of act. After we carefully examine the actual effects of each act—including its contribution to triggering a threshold—we divide up the acts into homogeneous subclasses. Each of these subclasses, being homogeneous (i.e., made up of relevantly similar acts), must, by Lyons's definitions, be linear. Hence, G must equal $n \times S$ for each subclass of acts. So after we give all due credit for thresholds and other variations in effects brought about by the causal context offered by the behavior of others, we arrive at a series of classes (or subclasses) of acts for which $G = N \times S$ (for purposes of moral generalizations).

Lyons argued, of course, that because G always equals $N \times S$ for relevantly similar acts, equivalence between S (the individual consequences) and G (the generalized consequences) must be guaranteed. As we saw, he claimed that because G and S are "proportional," by definition, they cannot differ in moral quality.

Yet this conclusion does not hold at the large scale—given our assumption of a cutoff for triviality. For a large enough number of acts—whose individual consequences are so trivial that they must be morally indifferent—may, nevertheless, produce total consequences that are morally significant. Linearity may hold, but N may be so large that even though G is significant, a $1/N$ share of G is so small as to be insignificant or below the cutoff for triviality.

Consider acts performed within a general pattern that involves threshold effects. Lyons thought that we might arrive at the impression of non-equivalence by counting the threshold effects in the generalized consequences (G) but failing to count them in the individual consequences (S) because we viewed the act "in vacuo," i.e., in isolation from the behavior of others. Hence we might believe that everyone's walking on the grass produced significant consequences but that any individual act of walking on the grass (performed within such a general context) was trivial. Or we might believe that everyone's voting produced significant consequences but that my individual vote must be meaningless.

Now Lyons's claim is that once we reckon in these threshold effects, equivalence must be restored. But whether or not this is the case depends on how *many* persons are credited with equal ($1/N$) shares of the significant threshold effect. If N is large enough, it may be the case that G is significant but S—even when credited with $1/N$ of the threshold effect—may still be so small as to be insignificant. In other words, the fact that S is $1/N$ of G does not entail that the individual and generalized consequences must support the same moral conclusions. Provided that sufficiently trivial effects are regarded as insufficient to determine obligations, S may be so small that it falls within the zone of indifference, even though G is large enough to be morally significant (i.e., fall within the zone of moral requirement).

In fact, this is a plausible interpretation of the cases already discussed. It may take a very large number of people similarly walking on the grass to ruin it. Or it may take a very large number of people voting for a given candidate if he is to win a major election. If these acts form homogeneous classes, then by Lyons's definitions, each individual act must be credited with $1/N$ of the total consequences, G. Even with the threshold effects counted in, our everyday perception may be correct that the *individual* consequences of these acts are trivial.

Or consider our earlier problem of paying taxes. In his "dialogue" between a "defaulter" and a "moralist," Strang arms the former with this argument:

> The exchequer would no more miss my £100 if *everyone* evaded than they would if only I evaded. They wouldn't miss anyone's individual evasion. What they would miss would be the aggregate £1,000,000,000 or so, and that isn't my default or yours or anyone's.[2]

In other words, even in the context of a general pattern of others doing the same, the individual consequences would be trivial in this case. In terms of the individual consequences of the act, we are told "each person's grounds for evasion would still be as valid as they would have been if he had been the only evader and no disaster had ensued." While such total effects would rightly influence our judgment of the *generalized*

---

2. Colin Strang, "What If Everyone Did That?" in Thomson and Dworkin, eds., *Ethics*, pp. 151–62. The quotation is from p. 155.

consequences, they must leave unaffected our evaluation of the tiny *individual* consequences of the act. By the latter criterion, it may even be irrational to pay when others are defaulting:

> none of the defaulters would be to blame for the disaster—and certainly not one of them would blame himself: on the contrary, each one would argue that had he paid he would have been the only one to pay and thus lost his £100 without doing himself or anyone else any good. He would have been a "mug" to pay.[3]

Ewing applied this same interpretation to the tax-evasion problem and extended it to military service and voting, as well. He considered the argument that it might be wrong to evade taxes "if the number of evasions were ever so great as seriously to threaten the national revenue." But he concluded that the existence of such a general pattern would not change our evaluation of the *individual* consequences of the act:

> it would still remain true that the amount I pay would not make any appreciable difference to the situation, and the same would apply to the other cases, military service and voting, so I should still be under an obligation to do something that did no appreciable good.[4]

Or consider our rationing cases. If an individual uses extra water or electicity during a draught or a power shortage it is plausible for him to regard his tiny transgression as an insignificant "drop in the bucket." He may reason: "The little drop I need won't make any difference and no one will know." Or: "Just my small electric fire won't count."[5] Such arguments based on *individual* consequences, furthermore, do not seem to be affected by the retort that if enough others

---

3. Ibid.
4. Ewing, "What Would Happen?" pp. 23–24.
5. Stout, "But Suppose Everyone Did the Same," p. 16.

are actually doing the same, the *total* results will be disastrous. For even if others are not conserving according to the ration, the added consequences of one more similar act will not significantly add to the total.

For these cases, after we give every individual act credit for its share in producing the collective effect, it is still plausible to believe that the act will have *negligible* individual consequences—even though the collective effects of everyone's doing the same are significant.

Of course, this possibility only arises at the large scale. That is, a *small* number of trivial acts cannot amount, collectively, to significant effects. An individually insignificant S, if multiplied by a small N, can be assumed to yield a similarly insignificant G. N must be large if it is to magnify the trivial to a level of moral significance—as did Broad's "microscope." Or, put another way, only if a significant G is equally shared among a large enough number of acts can its corresponding individual consequences fall below any given cutoff for triviality. No matter how significant the collective consequences, G, if it is apportioned among a large enough number of individual acts, they may each fall below the cutoff.

Of course, this argument depends upon assuming the cutoff for triviality. Lyons does not explicitly discuss the question; hence he could avoid our conclusion by denying that assumption. He would be forced, as a result, to count every trivial effect as sufficient to determine an act as right or wrong. As we saw in section 13, such a position would sacrifice the robust zone of indifference.

In fact, Lyons implicitly appeals to such a cutoff in his argument. For he talks about apparent nonequivalence resulting when we classify together acts that have "negligible" effects with those that have "appreciable" effects. That acts which have negligible effects should be classified as "indifferent" is not in dispute. The only question at issue is the class within which such acts should fall for purposes of generalization.

Furthermore, Lyons talks about the behavior of others as a factor that "enlarges" or increases actually extant effects of a morally indifferent act. There is no question of such acts having, literally, no morally relevant effects. Rather "negligible" effects are increased to a level of moral significance once the threshold is counted in. But surely whether this occurs depends upon *how widely shared* is the credit for the significant threshold effects.

Lyons explains how the "qualitative change" comes about:

> The *qualitative change* from the negligible to the *appreciable,* and in general, the *accumulation, expansion,* and *enhancement of effects* [italics added] depend upon this factor, that is, upon *how general* the practice is [italics in original].[6]

As this passage implies, each act may be regarded as having *some* consequences of the relevant kind, for each act contributes to "the accumulation, expansion and enhancement of effects." Each such act is not, then, *totally* lacking in effects but its individual contribution is, rather, "negligible." The accumulation of such insignificant effects may, on the other hand, add up to an amount that is "appreciable." The fact that this qualitative change is meant to occur through the addition (i.e., "accumulation") of individually insignificant—but still existing—contributions implies the kind of cutoff for triviality we have assumed. Yet, as we have seen, this cutoff would imply cases of non-equivalence at the large scale. For if a significant G is distributed widely enough within a linear class, $1/N$ of G may be small enough to fall below any given cutoff we may wish to define.

Where, precisely, this cutoff turns out to be is not a question we need decide here. So long as the theoretical applicability of *some* cutoff is accepted, cases of non-equivalence

---

6. Lyons, *Forms and Limits,* p. 72.

arise. For however low we set the cutoff, a large enough number of relevantly similar acts could share credit for a significant total, G, and fall below the cutoff.

Now whether or not Lyons accepts the cutoff for triviality, my primary purpose here has not been to offer counterexamples to his argument. For by denying the cutoff he could avoid cases of non-equivalence. Denying the cutoff would, of course, have further implications that many have regarded as absurd. But one could consistently take such a position.

If Lyons were to avoid this argument by denying the cutoff for triviality, he would take his position outside the consensus of moral assumptions which define the subject of this book. For he could not (a) maintain a utilitarian position and (b) deny the cutoff for triviality without also (c) denying the robust sphere of indifference. Counting every trivial effect as sufficient to support classification of actions as right or wrong, good or bad (in the sense of determining moral requirements), would quickly trivialize the sphere of indifference. No effect or risk, however small, could be neglected. What proportion of our normally robust sphere of permissibly free personal choice could withstand consistent application of such scrutiny of every tiny effect?

But this is only the beginning of the problem facing the sphere of indifference. For whether or not all of the examples discussed in this section are treated as technical cases of non-equivalence, they exemplify the power of "magnification" (to use Broad's analogy) of the generalization argument at the large scale. In other words, whether or not the cutoff for triviality is accepted, it should be clear that a normally robust sphere of indifference could not withstand consistent applications of the generalization argument at the large scale. Few actions do not produce *some* discernible effects which, if magnified (linearly or *via* thresholds[7]) by *enough* others, could not be imagined to produce aggregate effects of

---

7. See the analysis of Kantian generalization in the next section for

sufficient moral significance to turn them into moral questions. Before pursuing this threat to the sphere of indifference in more detail, let us extend our results thus far to some other varieties of generalization.

Lyons attempt to overcome F's generalization problem

① Strict Utilitarianism means evaluating likely consequences of identical acts

② An act can't be both morally trivial on ind. level + significant on general level.

③ This so, as the distinction between them is clarified when we look at likely effects of others action. (i.e. we can tell if our walking on grass is likely to be harmful or not) (THRESHHOLD.)

④ ∴ An act is individually trivial when we see a negligible effect of its taking place + significant when we can see a significant effect of its taking place.

F. rejects this - over large scale - many acts which our normal moral sense tells us are trivial have significant consequences.

Strict utilitarianism fails to overcome generalization problem on large scale while maintaining of moral sense understanding (i.e. sphere of indifference, etc.)

---

cases where hypothetical (in addition to actual) threshold effects produce such magnification.

16. Kantian Generalization

According to the utilitarian version of generalization, if an act is insignificant because it is isolated, its generalization can only range over other acts that are similarly insignificant—and hence similarly isolated.

If the isolated act of walking on the grass, or of not voting, or of defaulting on one's taxes does no harm because it is isolated, then its generalization can only bid us to envision others doing the "same"—namely, walking on the grass, not voting, or defaulting on one's taxes—when most others do not.

But there is another form of the generalization argument that is not encumbered by these utilitarian restrictions. It would include hypothetical threshold effects even when the individual act does not actually contribute to such a threshold. For it would have us imagine the hypothetical consequences of so many walking on the grass that it is ruined, of so many not voting that the institutions of democracy somehow collapse, of so many defaulting on their taxes that the government goes bankrupt. According to this version, our obligations are not affected by the actual behavior of others. The point of this kind of generalization is to evaluate an act under a morally appropriate—but hypothetical—supposition.

This form of argument is familiar. In fact, Lyons introduces the notion of generalization with an example of it at the beginning of the book. Should a passerby pick an apple from an orchard? The passerby should reason:

if everyone did the same, if every passer-by picked as he chose, this grower (or perhaps all growers) would suffer irretrievable losses.[1]

Clearly, "everyone" here is a hypothetical number large enough to pick the orchard bare. It is not the number who could pick an apple—provided that it was one of only a few isolated and insignificant cases. The fact that others are not doing it, so no actual harm results, is beside the point. As Marcus Singer notes about this form of generalization:

> It is simply irrelevant to reply, "Not everyone *will* do it." It may be the case, and in most cases almost certainly is, that not everyone will do the act in question; but the generalization argument in no way denies this.[2]

On this view, the fact that others are doing their duty does not provide me with an excuse not to. Or the fact that they are not doing their duty does not provide me with a reason for not doing so as well. R. B. Brandt, for example, comments on a "rationing" problem (where a "Frenchman" wishes to take more than his share of electricity in wartime England):

> a qualified person would not count it as a special reason (for not obeying) that one happens to know that all others are obeying cheerfully.[3]

Colin Strang offers the same conclusion with regard to the tax evader; he cannot refuse on the ground that others are paying because "there must always be a *reason* for treating people differently."[4]

Even though we know that most others will pay their taxes—so my not doing so will have no bad consequences (as-

---

1. Lyons, *Forms and Limits of Utilitarianism,* p. 2.
2. Marcus Singer, *Generalization in Ethics,* p. 90.
3. R. B. Brandt, *Ethical Theory* (Englewood Cliffs, N.J.: Prentice-Hall, 1959) p. 404.
4. Strang, "What If Everyone Did That?" p. 158.

suming that I can somehow get away with it)—the actual insignificance of the act resulting from its isolation is not regarded as a relevant factor. As Ewing notes in discussing the same example:

> I think we should all hold the [tax evader's] plea to be unjustified, and the reason is surely not that the calculation as to the effect of the particular act of paying one's tax is wrong, but that, if the argument were admitted in one case, it would have to be admitted in all, and then no taxes would be paid by anybody, a situation which ultimately would have disastrous results.[5]

So if an act *would have* morally significant threshold effects if it were performed by enough others, this form of generalization would count in the threshold effects—whether or not there is, in fact, an actual pattern of enough others doing likewise to trigger the threshold. This strategy of argument, which we have labeled Kantian,[6] encounters implications at the large scale parallel to those that apply to Lyons's strategy of "utilitarian" generalization.

For the point of this alternative version is to ignore the *actual* effects of the act that depend upon the behavior of others. If these actual effects are ignored for the generalized consequences, they should similarly be ignored for the individual consequences. For both criteria must be treated "analogously" under the same assumptions. So if we count a purely

---

5. Ewing, "What Would Happen?" p. 17. It is worth noting the obvious parallel between these cases and the "large group" cases for which Mancur Olson argues that it is (egoistically) rational to be a "free-rider." In the Olson cases, the individual can reason that he will get the public good in any case and will be better off if he gets out of contributing his share. For these cases, the generalization argument has a clear moral relevance—although it need have no effect on agents who are "rational" merely in the economic sense. See Mancur Olson, *The Logic of Collective Action* (New York: Shocken Books, 1968), chapters 1 and 2. For a sophisticated critique and reconstruction of Olson's argument, see Russell Hardin, *Collective Action* (Baltimore: Johns Hopkins, forthcoming).

6. See footnote 9, section 12, above.

hypothetical general pattern of conduct (which triggers threshold effects) in the generalized consequences, we should also count those same hypothetical threshold effects in the individual consequences.

The moral force of treating the individual consequences in this way can be seen from an example of Strang's:

> If two are needed to launch and man the lifeboat, the lone volunteer can only stand and wait: *he also* serves. The least a man can do is offer and hold himself ready, though sometimes it is also the most he can do [italics in original].[7]

The lone volunteer's act viewed in utilitarian terms has negligible consequences; without a second volunteer, the act of the first makes no actual contribution to the lifesaving effort. But viewed under the Kantian strategy, he can reason that *if* everyone were to do as he did, the lifeboat could be launched and lives could be saved. The generalized consequences of the act under this (morally relevant) supposition are thus significant. But what of the individual consequences? If these were to be viewed in utilitarian terms, it is clear that no significant individual consequences would be involved (for the man offering to man the lifeboat turns out to accomplish nothing). Furthermore, if these were to be viewed in isolation (as Lyons says, "*in vacuo*")—without taking into account the hypothesized threshold effects that would follow *if others were to act in accordance with the generalization*, then no significant consequences would be involved.

However, if the same counterfactual but morally relevant supposition is applied to both the generalized and the individual consequences—namely, that others also do their duty as determined by the generalization—then we can apply Lyons's formula $G = N \times S$ just as before. If we count a hypothetical threshold in G then we should also count it in

---

7. Strang, "What If Everyone?" pp. 160–61.

the analogous account of S. The individual who volunteers
for the lifeboat does his bit. It turns out that his act was insignificant *because* others did not do theirs. If, however,
everyone had done his duty, the volunteer's act would have
been significant. If this hypothetical supposition is reckoned
into the generalized consequences for this distinctly un-
utilitarian strategy of argument, then it should also be reckoned into the analogous individual consequences.

Of course, the generalized consequences resulting from
this Kantian strategy of generalization may differ from the individual consequences of the act considered in *utilitarian*
terms (permitting the actual behavior of others into the calculation of consequences). But the Kantian generalization may,
similarly, differ from the utilitarian generalization of the
same act. And the account of *individual* consequences
analogous to this Kantian form of generalization may also
conflict with a strictly utilitarian account of the corresponding individual consequences. But this is simply to say that
Kantian and utilitarian morality conflict. The conflict does
not depend upon the difference in structure between the
generalized- and individual-consequences principles.

So this Kantian strategy of argument would count a morally significant but *hypothetical* general pattern of conduct in
the "G" of Lyons's formula. Counting in the same counterfactual supposition about the behavior of others in S, G still
equals $N \times S$. This means that only when N is large enough
can G be significant but S be so small as to be morally trivial.

As we saw earlier, at the large scale it might be plausible
for me to reason that everyone's walking on the grass would
ruin it—but even if everyone else *did* walk on the grass, the
little bit *my* walking would add to the damage would make no
significant difference. In other words, even under the
hypothetical supposition that walking on the grass became a
general practice, the individual consequences my act would
add could still turn out to be trivial. Similar reasoning applies
to the tax defaulter. Suppose, knowing that most people will

in fact pay their taxes, he adopts the Kantian strategy of generalization and envisions the hypothetical consequences of everyone's not paying taxes. Hence, he envisions the hypothetical threshold effect of the government's going bankrupt. He can still reason, however, that even *if* so many others defaulted that the government went bankrupt, the little bit he adds would make no difference. The individual consequences of his act, judged in the context of such a hypothetical general pattern, could still turn out to be insignificant. It should be clear that counting in hypothetical threshold effects does not affect the possibilities for conflicting moral conclusions we encountered earlier at the large scale.

It should be noted, however, that this strategy of argument encounters a new difficulty that does not apply to the utilitarian form of generalization. Which of the various possible hypothetical general patterns should be selected? For many acts have the property that they may be connected to more than one hypothetical threshold effect.

Should the consequences of my not voting for candidate X be generalized to follow from all supporters of candidate X not voting, or to all voters in the election not voting? The generalized consequences of the former act include candidate X losing the election; the generalized consequences of the latter act include an undermining of the entire electoral system and perhaps some sort of indeterminate outcome to the election. Our difficulty is that the same act might be plausibly generalized in either way.

Broad argues that problems of this kind constitute "a special difficulty which affects the argument from false universalization." Consider two countries, A and B, at war. If "a citizen of A refuses to join his army" should this act be generalized over all members of country A or over all members of countries A *and* B?

If he means the latter, it is clear that the very best results would follow if everyone followed his example, for then both A and B would necessarily retain their prosperity.[8]

If everyone in *both* countries refused to join the army, then peace would result. But if everyone in country A alone refused, the victory of country B would result.

It should be obvious that this problem does not affect our earlier, utilitarian form of generalization. On that version there is no question of choosing between alternative *hypothetical* threshold effects or general patterns. For only *actual* threshold effects are counted on the strictly utilitarian interpretation.

This is a special difficulty, in other words, which applies to our second, Kantian form of generalization. Kant, of course, offered a solution to the problem—we are to generalize the "maxim" or actual subjective principle upon which the agent acts. Some modern neo-Kantians, such as Onora Nell, have argued that this is an adequate solution to the problem.[9]

However, this "solution" is not without difficulties. It introduces a radical indeterminacy into our evaluation of any given action. For the generalization would then be determined by the actual intentions of the agent. Does the "maxim" of his action include the intention that he avoid voting for candidate X? If so, the hypothetical generalization would range over the abstention of all supporters of X. Or is it just not voting, per se. If so, then all of those who would vote are to be imagined staying home. Does the agent actually differentiate these possibilities clearly? Suppose he is unsure how to formulate his intention. The generalization argument will confront him with sharply differing evaluations, depending upon how, precisely, he formulates his subjective principle of action.

---

8. Broad, "On the Function of False Hypothesis in Ethics," p. 391.

9. Onora Nell, *Acting on Principle: An Essay on Kantian Ethics* (New York: Columbia University Press, 1975), chapters 2 and 3.

Or suppose that his subjective principle of action makes essential reference to the act's *not* triggering a threshold. It may be part of my principle of action, in walking on the grass, that I *not* contribute to any threshold effects. I may intend for the act to be insignificant and, for that reason, perform it in an isolated context. Is the generalization therefore limited to other acts that are similarly insignificant? If so, then the distinctive moral force of the Kantian version would be trivialized and its implications would be reduced, in such cases, to those of the utilitarian version.

Clearly, a complete account of Kantian generalization would require a solution to this problem of competing descriptions. Different descriptions of the same act, sometimes only slightly different formulations of apparently similar intentions, may lead to quite different generalizations of "everybody doing the same."

My intention, however, is not to offer any particular solution to this problem. Rather, my point is that any such account is subject to problems of scale—in the evaluation of morally significant consequences—which parallel those that apply to utilitarian generalization.

17. When Everyone Actually Does the Same

The principles of generalization just discussed, while a prominent part of our ordinary moral conceptions, are also subject to a familiar, commonsense objection. Broad identified the problem in this way:

> The paradox is this. We are asked to believe that the rightness or wrongness of many of our actions depends on the probable consequences, not of what we know to be true, but of what we know to be false. For, in practically every case where we consider what would happen if everybody acted as we propose to act, we know as surely as we can know anything that is not *a priori*, that by no means will everybody act in this way.[1]

Proponents of this principle appear committed to "the extraordinary position that it is only the consequences of what we know to be false that are ethically relevant, whereas the consequences of what we know to be true are wholly unimportant." A bachelor, for example, who wishes to remain unmarried might admit, nevertheless, that if everyone refused to marry, bad consequences would result. Yet since "there is not the least prospect of everybody refusing to marry or even of so many people remaining unmarried as to lead to the consequences which they agree would be bad,"[2] it does not seem

---

1. Broad, "On the Function of False Hypothesis in Ethics," pp. 377–78.
2. Ibid.

rational for Broad's solitary bachelor to be required to marry because of such purely hypothetical consequences.

The first thing to notice about this example is that it does not apply to the generalization argument, *per se*, but only to some particular versions of it. The strictly utilitarian version refined by Lyons, for example, would not have this result. Although the utilitarian form of generalization does indeed require us to envision hypothetical consequences, those consequences depend crucially on what is considered the "same act." Broad's solitary bachelor does no actual harm by not marrying, for he avoids marrying in a causal context of at least enough others marrying that the human race will remain well populated (if not overpopulated). So the utilitarian description of the act to be generalized must include the proviso that the act has no actual bad consequences *because* it is relatively isolated. The generalization of *that* act can only range over a number of others who could do the "same" with the same consequences. So the generalization must envisage only those not marrying who, like the solitary bachelor, could do so without causing any harm.

Although utilitarian generalization is immune from the absurdities of this particular example, it bids us, nevertheless, to envision hypothetical consequences. Like the Kantian form of generalization, it would have us regulate our conduct according to our evaluation of a counterfactual supposition, What *if* everyone were to do the same? Both of these versions of the generalization argument may be called *hypothetical* generalizations, for they do not depend upon any factual claim that others *are* actually doing the same. This is the form of the argument that has been most influential and it is the one that has concerned us thus far.

However, the difficulties with generalization arguments at the large scale are not dependent upon the hypothetical character of the test. There are also varieties of the argument that require an *actual* pattern[3] of people generally performing

---

3. I use the term "pattern" rather than "practice" here in order to in-

the action if the consequences of "everybody doing the same" are to be ethically relevant. Let us call this the *actual consequences* version of the generalization argument, as follows:

ACTUAL CONSEQUENCES VERSION OF GENERALIZATION: *A sufficient condition for an act's being morally required (positively or negatively) is the moral significance of a general pattern of others actually doing the same.*

Hence, we can consider three distinct versions of the generalization argument: The first two, the Kantian and utilitarian varieties, are hypothetical in form. They ask us to regulate our conduct by the moral significance of a supposition that may be counterfactual, i.e., What if other did the same? The third version is restricted to the evaluation of cases where others *actually* do the same. It is, thus, immune to Broad's objection. All three of these versions are problematical at the large scale. Whichever version we choose, we encounter special difficulties when large enough numbers are involved.

Even for an actual pattern of conduct, if $G = N \times S$, then the

---

clude two varieties: (a) actual *patterns* where the participants may or may not *intend* to participate in a common undertaking for the shared and explicit purpose of producing certain aggregate consequences, (b) actual moral *practices* where the participants do so intend (the term "rule utilitarianism" is sometimes restricted to this latter version). Note that our food examples (later in this section) would apply only to *a*; however, all of the examples used in the "overload" argument in the next section apply to both *a* and *b*. They are all good causes supported by actual practices. I have used the more general category here (actual patterns) in order to capture *both* varieties of the argument.

This principle might also be formulated comparatively so as to determine moral requirements depending upon how the moral significance of a general pattern compared to that of other general patterns available to the same agent. Such a comparative version would clearly not affect the vulnerability of this principle to overload problems. After performing the act of greatest comparative significance, the agent would then be vulnerable to the request that he perform the act of next greatest, and then the act of next greatest, and so on. The robust sphere of indifference would give way before any thoroughgoing attempt to fulfill enough such obligations seriatim.

only possibility for conflicting moral conclusions is for S to be so tiny in its effects as to be below the cutoff for triviality—even though N is so large that G, in aggregate, is significant. The fact that G must actually result for the principle to be brought into play does not affect our previous analysis. Conflicting moral conclusions between G and S are, once more, only possible at the large scale.

In addition to such problems of non-equivalence, this principle is also clearly vulnerable to overload. If applied consistently at the large scale, the actual consequences version of generalization—like the hypothetical versions already considered—would pervasively moralize many trivial aspects of our everyday lives. For many aspects of life—which we customarily place within the zone of indifference—are typical in that they are shared by millions of others. In aggregate, these actions may have morally significant actual effects even though their individual consequences are so small that we would be correct to place them below the cutoff for triviality.

Consider, for example, the question of food. In a world where famine and malnutrition are common, we in the Western developed countries commonly indulge in the wasteful practice of eating meat. We feed 78 percent of all our grain to cattle to produce meat. For beef and veal it takes "21 pounds of protein in the form of grain to get back one pound in the form of meat."[4] Hence, most of us commonly engage in, and help to support, a kind of conduct that, in aggregate, is extremely wasteful of the world's precious food resources.

Am I, therefore, morally wrong to eat meat? Advocates of vegetarianism admit that if I give up meat my *individual* effect on the world food situation will be trivial. But they are willing to moralize the issue, nevertheless, as in this advertisement for a vegetarian cookbook in the *New Haven Advocate:*

---

4. James Rachels, "Vegetarianism and the Other Weight Problem," in Aiken and LaFollette, eds., *World Hunger and Moral Obligation*, pp. 180–93. The quotation is from p. 185.

Cooking without meat will not guarantee an end to world
hunger. It will mean that you won't be eating meat. Meat,
especially beef, wastes valuable grains when it is produced....you won't end all hunger, but *you will be helping to fight hunger if you cook vegetarian* [emphasis ad-
ded].

Here the actual, wasteful consequences of eating meat
turn the issue into a moral one.[5] It is not merely the individual
consequences (which are admittedly minuscule) but the fact
that the general practice of eating meat has, in aggregate, such
significant effects on the world food situation.

Yet any individual who tries to determine whether he
should eat meat faces the same difficulty at the large scale that
we have already encountered with the hypothetical forms of
generalization. Although this general pattern of conduct may,
in aggregate, produce significant effects, any individual's
contribution to them must be so small as to be negligible.
Aside from the factual quibbles that might be offered against
advocates of vegetarianism, if I am contributing to world
hunger by eating meat, that contribution must be extremely
negligible. But the generalized consequences of everyone's
actually doing the same may have, in aggregate, the significant consequences alleged. Am I to guide my conduct by
the trivial individual consequences or by the collectively significant aggregate consequences of everyone's actually doing
the same? If I consistently guide my conduct by G, acts with
small individual consequences will be raised to the level of
moral requirement. But if, on the other hand, I were to guide it
by S, then an important objection against the free-rider and

---

5. Rachels makes a similar argument (about saving both food and ani-
mals): "One consumer's behavior by itself, cannot have a noticeable impact
on an industry as vast as the meat business. However, it is important to see
one's behavior in a wider context. There are already millions of vegetarians,
and because they don't eat meat there *is* less cruelty than there otherwise
would be." (Ibid., p. 192.)

the tax defaulter would be lost. For in our previous applications of generalization against the free-rider, it is worth noting that the actual consequences version of generalization would apply just as did the hypothetical versions. For our examples assumed an actual pattern of others generally voting, of others generally paying their taxes, of others generally staying off the lawn. These actual patterns, in aggregate, produce morally significant consequences. These collectively significant consequences provide an argument against the free-rider, who would like to get out of taking the time to vote, to get out of paying his share of taxes, and to be permitted to walk on the lawn—whereas most others do not do likewise.

Hence, with the actual consequences version of generalization, we face the same dilemma that we encountered with the hypothetical forms of the argument. At the large scale, if we apply the principle of generalized consequences, we magnify to a level of moral significance acts that are, in their individual consequences, clearly trivial. On the other hand, if we refrain from applying the principle of generalized consequences, we lose the argument that has traditionally proven most powerful against the free-rider, the defaulter, the nonvoter.

18. The Overload of Obligations

In discussing various principles of generalization, our focus thus far has been on problems of non-equivalence. It should be evident, however, that this analysis has implications for any normally robust sphere of indifference. Consistent compliance with a principle of generalization, whether the hypothetical or actual consequences version, will routinely overwhelm an individual with moral requirements.

If this is true of the actual consequences version of generalization, then it must also be true for the two hypothetical versions. For all cases of moral significance for the actual consequences version are included within the cases for which the hypothetical versions determine moral requirements. The principles that determine moral requirements under the supposition, What *if* others did the same? include the cases in which others actually *do* the "same." The distinctive feature of the hypothetical versions is that they moralize, in addition, many apparently trivial actions by asking us to envision the consequences that *would* result if others were to do likewise. Hence, if the actual consequences version leads to overload under realistic conditions, then the other two, hypothetical versions must also—for they will place many additional actions within the sphere of moral requirement.

As I sort through my desk while I write this essay, I see appeals for money, time, or effort from the following organizations:

CARE

Children, Inc. (an adoption program asking for contributions of $15 a month)

The United Jewish Appeal

The Yale Alumni Fund

Common Cause

Amnesty International

Environmental Action

The United Way

John Anderson's Presidential Campaign

The United Negro College Fund

The Democratic Socialist Organizing Committee

Connecticut Public Television

The Infant Formula Action Coalition (or "infact" for the boycott of Nestlé products)

The Southern Coalition on Jails and Prisons, Inc.

UNICEF (The United Nation's Children's Fund)

The Connecticut Lung Association

The American Friends of Cambridge University

The Newington Children's Hospital

This is a random, variegated list of appeals that have been sent to me over the last few days. It should be obvious that if I made even the slightest effort to *seek out* good causes, I could construct a list many hundreds of times this length. Each of us, depending on our own moral and political predilections, would include different organizations and causes on any such list. The general point should be obvious. Consistent compliance with the nonhypothetical, actual consequences version of generalization would commit us to an overload of obligations sufficient to overwhelm the basic structure. For all of these good causes have actual—not hypothetical—groups of many persons actively engaged. Those groups are, I have no doubt, doing good work. But if their good efforts are sufficient to determine obligations for *me*, the number of such obligations that must, out of consistency, be admitted will easily, under realistic conditions, overwhelm both the robust sphere of indifference and, in all likelihood, the cutoff for heroism. For if I must attempt to conform to *all* of these obligations, that would seem a sacrifice great enough to add up to a supererogatory pattern of conduct—it would amount to a renunciation of an entire way of life, one whose permissibility most of us take for granted.

The difficulty is merely an instance of the argument we developed in part I. Each of these principles of generalization is both general and positive in form. It determines requirements for me or for anyone else of ordinary capacities, regardless of my previous actions, history, or efforts—including any actions directed at limiting my obligations to a manageable few. It can obligate me despite the absence of promises, consent, contracts, kinship, or any other voluntary acts or particular roles that would differentiate me from others and bind me, especially, to perform the action. So long as the specified conditions occur for an obligation-determining situation (in this case, enough others actually, or hypothetically, doing the same), I am required, by the principle, to act. And when there are enough obligation-determining situations of this kind, overload is inescapable. My point here is that the empirical conditions for overload for these particular principles of obligation (the three versions of generalization just discussed) occur routinely in our daily lives. Such general principles, when consistently applied to familiar conditions in the world, will quickly overwhelm any normally robust sphere of indifference and any reasonable cutoff for heroism.

These examples also serve to insulate the argument from another objection. For it might be argued that the food example in the last section failed to distinguish "rule utilitarian" patterns from other general patterns of behavior. We feed ourselves without any explicit intention to produce the *aggregate* consequences referred to in the principle. Suppose we distinguished a version of actual consequences generalization which required that the actual pattern of behavior be *explicitly undertaken* to produce (or avoid) good or bad aggregate consequences. In other words, the general pattern must be a moral *practice*. This might be formulated as follows:

> RULE UTILITARIAN VERSION OF ACTUAL CONSEQUENCES: *A sufficient condition for an act's being morally required (positively or negatively) is the significance of a general moral practice of others actually doing the same.*

The prescriptions justified by this restricted version are all *included* in the prescriptions supported by the broader version of *actual consequences generalization* and by the two hypothetical versions. However, even this restricted version leads routinely to overload. Note that all of the examples discussed in this section involve actual patterns of behavior explicitly undertaken to produce aggregate good consequences. They all involve moral practices in the sense just defined. The restriction of the argument to this variant of rule utilitarianism would not insulate us from overload, since the number of actual good causes with actual cadres of workers intending to bring about desirable aggregate effects is easily sufficient to produce overload for any of us.

It is enough that this conclusion easily follows for these actual consequences versions of generalizations. Consider the additional pressure brought by the hypothetical versions. What trivial areas of life could withstand elevation to the level of moral seriousness (and of obligation) if enlarged by Broad's "microscope" at a sufficiently high level of magnification? We have already seen the intrusion of morality into questions of individual diet—an area that most of us would normally regard as safely within the sphere of indifference. Surely our occupations, our family life, our choices of residences, our allocations of leisure time, would all become subject to a host of moral requirements if these areas of life were persistently subjected to generalization arguments of the hypothetical variety. Even were we to avoid these additional intrusions on the sphere of indifference by sticking to the actual consequences version, the overload problem appears inescapable under realistic conditions. The dilemma we encountered in part 1 is not merely a theoretical puzzle. For these common moral principles—all of these varieties of generalization in addition to the principle of minimal altruism—the problem of overload arises routinely. If we are committed to these assumptions, we can only pretend to escape it by efforts to avoid thinking about the problem. The necessary ingredients are nothing more than the familiar conditions of everyday life. And the problem that results is a systematic challenge to the moral assumptions underlying the way most of us think—and live.

PART III:
Conclusion

19. The Central Dilemma

My central thesis is quite simple. Once stated, it seems obvious and almost self-evident. Yet, if explicitly faced, it stands as a challenge to the common moral assumptions that underlie the way most of us think and live.

Either we must give up some element of the basic structure of individual morality or we must give up general obligations. Otherwise, we must accept a breakdown in our fundamental assumptions. Such a breakdown would mean that we lack a coherent moral position. It would also provide continuing fuel for cynicism and hypocrisy. Hence, in examining the possible alternatives below, I will assume that this breakdown must be repaired, one way or another.

The inescapable dilemma arises from overload problems. As we have seen, depending on the precise formulation of a given principle of obligation, we may also face non-equivalence problems. Because overload problems are unavoidable, the essential dilemma reduces us to a few stark alternatives:

1a. the option of giving up the cutoff for heroism,
1b. the option of giving up the robust sphere of indifference,
1c. both of the above, or
2. the option of giving up principles of positive general obligation.

Let us explore each of these possibilities in turn.

1a. If we were to give up the cutoff for heroism, then there

153

would be no limits on the effort, risk, or sacrifice that could be demanded of us as a matter of duty or obligation. In effect, this is Peter Singer's solution to the famine relief problem. The entire way of life that most of us take for granted in the Western developed countries could then be condemned as immoral, provided that the world determined, as it easily does, enough obligations for us by a principle as innocent as minimal altruism. Even trivial sacrifices, as we have seen, can easily add up to heroic proportions under plausible conditions. If the cutoff for heroism were relinquished, then there would be no barrier to the conclusion that such enormous sacrifices could be demanded as a matter of obligation or duty. When we fail to live up to such demanding requirements we must then be morally blameworthy.

Perhaps Peter Singer is correct to draw such an extreme conclusion. I do not wish to decide this question here, one way or the other. I wish only to point out that if this horn of the dilemma were accepted, it would represent a massive revision in our common moral conceptions and in our common way of life. Although a coherent and defensible position would result from such a revision, we would all have a great deal of difficulty living up to it. For we would all then be required to make sacrifices that we now expect only of heroes or of saints.

1b. Alternatively, if we were to give up the robust sphere of indifference then we would accept the pervasive intrusion of morality into virtually every minor aspect of our daily lives. A recognizable form of life would result, but one that is distinctly foreign to modern secular Western culture. The result would be what Marcus Singer has called, in a provocative choice of terms, "moral fanaticism"—"the idea that no action is indifferent or trivial." Allowing for some hyperbole, he has identified the consternation most of us would feel at such a way of life. It is: "to suppose that every occasion of life gives rise to a moral problem, and that everything we do requires justification, and this is simply false. One who consistently thought so would die of moral perplexity."[1]

Perhaps this path of zealotry or "fanaticism" is the appropriate resolution. But opting for this horn of the dilemma would also amount to a very great revision in our common way of life. No longer would there be a significant sphere of action where I could, morally speaking, do as I please. Almost every action would be determined for me on moral grounds. The unstated presupposition of a kind of negative freedom would be lost.[2] Responsibility, blame, guilt, and questions of justification would become ever-present considerations, weighing on every choice and on every action. I do not presume to decide the question here of whether or not accepting this horn of the dilemma is the appropriate resolution. I wish only to point out that doing so would force us to reform our lives drastically or to accept requirements hypocritically that we would have great difficulty living up to.

1c. I include this alternative only to make explicit the fact that accepting either 1a or 1b might not, by itself, be sufficient. For depending upon the precise formulation of a principle, and depending upon the precise empirical circumstances, conflicts with both assumptions (the cutoff for heroism and the robust sphere of indifference) can be expected. Hence, arriving at a consistent and coherent moral position compatible with a principle of general obligation at the large scale may very well require *both* of the fundamental revisions just mentioned.

Arriving at such a position may very well require, in addition, some strategy for dealing with non-equivalence. For as we saw in detail in part II, depending on the precise formulation of a principle, conflicts with the unique classification

---

1. Marcus Singer, *Generalization in Ethics*, p. 185. Anthony Quinton makes a similar point and calls the result "a kind of moral totalitarianism." See Quinton, *Utilitarian Ethics*, p. 47.

2. See note 1, section 4, and the discussion corresponding to it.

assumption are also a routine occurrence at the large scale.[3]
Such cases of non-equivalence are, in their own way, pro-
foundly disturbing, for they lead to incompatible conclusions
about whether there is something we are required to do or
whether it is a discretionary matter. To accept that an act may
be simultaneously classified as both indifferent and required, or as both required and supererogatory, would be to
build such perplexities into the foundations of a moral system. Whether or not such a sacrifice in the unique classification assumption is required will depend on which principles
are under discussion. I have not included this option within
the horns of the central dilemma because it is not absolutely
inescapable. It looms, however, as a source of additional
difficulties at the large scale.

2. Avoiding 1*a*, 1*b*, and 1*c* would force us to give up principles of positive general obligation. Would we really be prepared to admit that there are not obligations to perform actions that we can demand of anyone else and that anyone else
can demand of us? Merely on the basis of common humanity,
are there not *some* things that we owe, even to a total stranger?

As we saw earlier, Nozick rejected all *positive* obligations. According to his position, I can do entirely as I please so
long as I refrain from certain "boundary crossings," certain
active violations of the "entitlements" of others. The rich
could not then be condemned for failing to assist the poor.
After all, by doing nothing they do not violate the entitlements or property rights of anyone else—even if the poor
starve to death as a result. According to this position, forced
redistribution, even for famine relief, must be condemned if it
violates the rights of the more fortunate. A general property of
such negative principles is that so long as we avoid violating
the stated prohibitions, we are free to do as we please. No

---

3. Of course, some possible principles of general obligation may be
formulated so as to produce non-equivalence at the small scale. My point in
part II was that principles which withstand non-equivalence at the small
scale become vulnerable to it merely as a result of increasing numbers (in one
or more of our three senses).

positive contributions would be required (except for the restitution of previous violations). Nozick admits that his position will seem "callous" to many. I mention this possibility only to point out that such a denial of positive obligations would avoid overload problems—but at the cost of a "callousness" that many of us would find morally unacceptable.

We have specified two requirements for obligations—they must be both positive and general. What would follow from a denial of general obligations?

If only special obligations were admitted, our obligations could be limited to those with whom we have close personal relations, those to whom we have consented or promised, and those who have some special claim on us because of a role or a public office we occupy. Such special obligation principles are thus largely immune to the slippery slope by which general obligations can so quickly overwhelm us.

Yet, to limit our obligations in this way would, I believe, involve a very great revision in our common moral conceptions. We would have to relinquish appeals to impartiality and fairness that many have identified with the moral point of view itself. Our account of general obligations in section 5 was simply an account of the kind of impartiality that has often been identified with the core notion of morality. The basic idea has been familiar since the Golden Rule. An agent performing an action should be able to view the obligation as unchanged, were he to change places with his recipients, or with any other persons who could perform the action. From such an objective perspective, we are led to consider other persons in the same way as we consider ourselves.

General obligations thus embody a familiar kind of impartiality. Furthermore, more specific models of impartiality or fairness that are commonly employed in arguing for substantive principles easily lead to principles of general obligation in the sense defined here. Consider the Golden Rule. If I conscientiously attempt to treat a starving refugee as I would wish him to treat me, I am compelled to admit a much more demanding principle of general obligation than our principle of minimal altruism. If I take seriously the idea of putting my-self in his place, some obligation to assist him is undeni-able—even though the starving refugee is, of course, a total stranger. And, as we have seen, even the weak principle of minimal altruism is capable of generating our dilemma at the large scale. The more demanding principles that I might eas-ily be led to adopt if I conscientiously applied the Golden Rule would only serve to intensify the dilemma.

Or consider Rawls's original position. Rawls argues that we should think of distribution for a just society from the hypothetical perspective of persons who know that they are to be members of it—but who know nothing in particular about themselves or about their society. Their choice is to be insu-lated from the contingencies that lead to biases and special pleading in ordinary life. I must imagine myself making a choice in the original position as if my enemy were to assign me my place.[4] Not knowing who I will turn out to be, I must take seriously the possibility that I will turn out to occupy the worst position.

Although Rawls develops his argument primarily for so-cial choice (principles for institutions in a just society) and not individual choice, he offers his book as *part* of a more general theory of "rightness as fairness" that should apply to individual as well as to social choice.[5] As we have seen, he does extend the argument to certain principles of "natural duty" including the "positive" one of "mutual aid." His as-sumptions, furthermore, provide the basis for a systematic account of individual morality. Richards has offered one ver-sion of such an extension.[6] Charles Beitz, furthermore, has applied the original position explicitly to international redis-tribution.[7] These extensions build on the idea that the origi-nal position embodies the moral point of view. Without

---

4. Rawls, *Theory of Justice*, p. 152.
5. Ibid., pp. 17, 111.
6. Richards, *A Theory of Reasons for Action*.
7. Beitz, *Political Philosophy, International Relations*, part 3.

elaborating the precise details of any particular effort to extend the argument, it should be obvious that from the original position there would be very great pressure indeed to admit general obligatons of a demanding kind.

I am to imagine myself choosing a moral principle out of self-interest from behind a "veil of ignorance" which, according to Rawls, makes it rational for me to take seriously the possibility that I will occupy the worst position. Clearly, I will wish to choose principles that ensure my survival and (at least) minimal well-being. The prospect of becoming a starving refugee provides a clear motivation for requiring substantial sacrifices from those who turn out to occupy the more fortunate positions.[8] It should be obvious that a principle of redistribution far more demanding than minimal altruism would be chosen in the original position. Yet even minimal altruism is sufficiently demanding, at the large scale, to produce our dilemma.

Another impartial moral perspective is the perfectly sympathetic spectator of the classical utilitarians. Such an ideal spectator can be imagined to reproduce in himself every pleasure and pain in the world. He will then, of course, prefer states of the world that maximize the net balance of pleasure over pain, of utility over disutility. This ideal spectator is the embodiment of an impersonal moral perspective in which each person's interests are accounted for in the same way and in which no one is left out. If such a perspective is adopted as the appropriate one for moral choice, it should be evident that general obligations of a demanding sort would be impossible to deny. None of the differentiating factors necessary for special obligatons is an admissible consideration for the ideal spectator. Each person is interchangeable with any other who has the same utility. And the general obligations that are

---

8. This argument holds even under Rawls's condition of only moderate scarcity. For that condition is compatible with sufficiently severe maldistribution of (only moderately scarce) resources that our famine problems may arise. See Rawls, *Theory of Justice*, p. 127.

appealing from such a perspective are all varieties of utilitarianism which lead easily to overload.

From all these impartial moral perspectives, general obligations follow directly. The precise character of the principles chosen will depend, of course, on the particular assumptions about interests imported into these various models of impartial moral choice. Yet if I must determine my obligations after I have accounted for the interests of a starving refugee in the same manner as I have accounted for my own, any plausible accounting of interests will lead me to require substantial assistance and redistribution. To deny such obligations would be to deny the claim of impartial perspectives according to which I must be prepared to put myself in the place of any other person. Perhaps such a revision is necessary but it would go to the heart of what has been commonly regarded as the constitutive features of morality itself.

Let us consider some principles that would avoid overload problems by failing to fulfill, in the first place, the requirements for general obligations. Familiar principles that would obligate us merely to our own families or to actions based on voluntary agreement or consent have already been mentioned. We might also imagine a kind of principle that violates the anonymity requirement in being *agent specific* in the sense that an agent's own previous history of conforming to the principle provides the basis for determining whether or not he must now do anything. Consider a weakened variant of minimal altruism that would fit within this category: "One is obligated to give *something* to prevent death and starvation, but how much and when is entirely up to individual discretion." So long as one engaged in an act of giving, at some time, one would fulfill this principle. Anyone who had not previously given anything would have a duty; but all those who had already given something would be exempt from all further requirements. If they then gave anything, in addition, that would be discretionary or supererogatory and not a matter of obligaton.

Kant's notion of an imperfect duty has sometimes been interpreted this loosely, but I am persuaded by more demanding interpretations that would place imperfect duties within, rather than outside of, the general obligation category.[9] In any case, this kind of weak moral requirement is very close to the way we often view the matter of charity: it is a private discretionary decision and so long as one does *something*, however small, one is largely immune from further criticism.

However appealing such a position might be for some matters of charity, if we were to limit our obligations *entirely*

---

9. Both Onora Nell (*Acting on Principle*, pp. 48–49) and Bruce Aune argue that Kant is inconsistent in his account of the perfect/imperfect distinction and that the best way to make sense of his position is to identify it—as Kant does at some points—with the distinction between "wide" and "narrow" duties. As Kant notes in the *Metaphysics of Morals*:

> a wide duty [i.e., to pursue certain ends] is not to be taken as a permission to make exceptions to the maxim of actions, but only as a permission to limit one maxim of duty by another (e.g., love of one's neighbor in general by love of one's parents)—a permission that actually widens the field for the practice of virtue. As the duty is wider, so man's obligation to action is more imperfect; but the closer to narrow duty (Law) he brings the maxim of observing his duty (in his attitude of will), so much the more perfect is his virtuous action. [Quoted in Bruce Aune, *Kant's Theory of Morals* (Princeton: Princeton University Press, 1979), p. 189.]

For wide duties, the discretion is not a matter of making exceptions, it is a matter of choosing alternative paths to the fulfillment of a given duty. Because such a duty singles out a class of alternatives that are required (compared to the other possibilities) and any one of which would fulfill the duty, such a wide duty can be positive in my sense. Aune argues against the interpretation, which Kant admittedly encourages at some points, that imperfect duties should be construed as permitting exceptions:

> Clearly, my duty to pursue obligatory ends does not allow exceptions "in the interest of inclination" either: I always have these obligations. Since perfect duties can be fulfilled in more than one way, it seems reasonable to say that the difference between them and imperfect duties is really one of degree and that the terms "narrow" and "wide" convey this difference better than "perfect" and "imperfect." A wide duty allows the agent considerable scope in deciding how to comply; a narrow duty limits this scope to a considerable extent. [Ibid., pp. 189–95.]

For our purposes, the relevant point is that "wide" or "imperfect" duties in this sense define moral requirements that are both "actual" and "positive."

to such a weak agent-specific conception, we would face all of the conflicts mentioned above with fundamental notions of moral impartiality. Could any of us imagine plausibly defending such a weak principle in applying the Golden Rule to the famine-relief problem? From any of the impartial perspectives discussed above, there would be overwhelming pressure to require that an agent do more than give something at some time entirely at his own discretion.

However, other agent-specific principles might be devised that are more demanding. Imagine, for example, a principle containing definite limits such as: "One is obligated to give 10 percent of one's income, and *no more*, to prevent death and starvation." According to such a principle, those who have given less than 10 percent are obligated to reach their quota; but anyone who has conformed to the stated limit cannot then be required to give a penny more. If the limit is designed so that it does not, by itself, violate the cutoff for heroism and the robust sphere of indifference, then such a one-shot obligation could conceivably avoid overload problems.

Yet, when further cases arise, there is a considerable burden facing such a principle. If I have given my 10 percent—and there are still more cases of starvation that could be avoided—why am I justified in refusing, when I can be confident that my additional contributions could still make a difference? If others are, in fact, not all doing their share so that further work remains to be done, the pressure on me to continue beyond any stated limits is very great indeed. At least when judged from any of the impartial perspectives mentioned above, any particular quota takes on the appearance of an ad hoc rationalization. Perhaps such a principle could be developed so that it was more defensible; it would

---

The kind of "discretion" that they permit is merely that between alternative paths to fulfill the same moral requirement. They would, then, be subject to our argument. For a similar interpretation of Kant, see Nell, *Acting on Principle,* pp. 48–49.

have to be accompanied, however, by an entire apparatus of justification designed to withstand such pressure. This apparatus remains to be developed.

Whether or not defensible versions of such principles could be developed, they would involve departures from the notion of general obligations employed here. No longer would the obligation remain unaffected were any person who could perform the action to exchange places with anyone else. For the idea of such agent-specific principles is that, depending on an agent's previous history of fulfilling obligations, he can be absolved from any further moral requirements. But were I to take seriously the requirement of impartial decision procedures, to put myself in the place of those affected by my actions (or inactions), it is hard to see how such a conception might be supported. From the perspective of a victim requiring famine relief, it is hard to see why X, in affluent circumstances, should not be required to make a further small sacrifice simply because X has already done *other* good deeds. If I have already helped victims in a fire, or taken boy scouts on an outing, or contributed to the Environmental Defense Fund, does that mean that, if faced with another case of easily amerliorated distress, I can simply ignore the appeal for help? Is it justifiable to claim, given my past history of good works, that I should now feel free to do nothing, that only others should be required to act? In a world of imperfect moral cooperation, others may not step in to do their share. Regardless of my history of action, it seems difficult for me then to avoid a share of the blame if I do nothing.

If we apply impartial decision procedures to this question of whether the previous sacrifices of an agent are relevant to his present obligations, we soon see the argument, from impartiality, against such agent-specific principles. For these impartial models are constructed so as to *disconnect* my past history of action from any direct bearing on the question. They require that we pose the problem either (a) in terms of a comparison of *marginal* effects (the change the act produces in my situation and in that of those helped) or (b) in terms of a consideration of *global* states (my overall situation and the overall situations of those helped after a given act).[10] Utilitarian decision procedures such as the impartial spectator would focus on *a*. So long as the marginal utility produced by the act exceeds its marginal disutility, there is an impulsion to require it (apart from questions about alternative acts that may produce even greater net gains or avoid even greater net losses). This was the basis for the slippery slope that led Singer, by a comparison of marginal effects, to advocate sacrifices for famine relief until we reached virtually the level of starving refugees ourselves:

> We ought to give until we reach the level of marginal utility—that is, the level at which, by giving more, I would cause as much suffering to myself or my dependents as I would relieve by my gift.[11]

The Golden Rule leads naturally to a similar comparison of marginal effects.[12] If I am to do unto a starving refugee as I

---

10. The consideration of global states may be comparative in that the overall situations of everyone affected by one act may be compared to the overall situations of everyone affected by some alternative act. If one of the acts considered is doing nothing, or maintaining the status quo, then a comparison of marginal changes (relative to that alternative) may come into the discussion.

11. Peter Singer, "Famine, Affluence and Morality," in Laslett and Fishkin, eds., *Philosophy, Politics and Society*, pp. 21–35. The quotation is from p. 33.

12. For philosophical discussions of the Golden Rule, see Hare, *Freedom and Reason*, especially chapter 9, Alan Gewirth, "The Golden Rule Rationalized," *Midwest Studies in Philosophy* 3 (1978), *Studies in Ethical Theory*, pp. 133–47; and his *Reason and Morality*. For a critique of Gewirth's employment of a principle closely related to the Golden Rule, see Adina Schwartz's review of *Reason and Morality* in *The Philosophical Review* 88 (1979): 654–56. For one particular interpretation of the Golden Rule that equates its implications with those of Rawls's original position, see Lawrence Kohlberg, "Justice as Reversibility" in Laslett and Fishkin, eds., *Philosophy, Politics and Society*, pp. 257–72. Despite the differences in these variants of the Golden Rule, they have all been employed by their authors in support of

would have him do unto me, were I in his position, the obvious disparity in marginal effects between my sacrifice and his benefit makes it very difficult to argue against the action in a manner consistent with the Golden Rule. I have only to imagine myself in his place and then compare the effects of the action viewed from mine to see the argument. Even if I have already made substantial sacrifices for other good causes in the past, the Golden Rule would have me compare only such effects at the margin. Past history would only be relevant indirectly, through its effect on the status quo from which the action is evaluated.

Rawls's original position, on the other hand, would lead us to frame the problem in terms of b, a consideration of global states. If Rawls is correct in claiming that his construction of the choice situation would lead us to take most seriously the possibility of being at the bottom,[13] then there would be a strong case for any actions that would raise the overall level at the bottom compared to the overall level of other positions. So long as the worst-off position is higher, there is a clear case for the change, regardless of the effects on all the other positions (except when one of these is reduced so far as to become the worst-off).

Whether we employ an impartial decision procedure focusing on global states or one focusing on marginal effects, these models have no provision for taking explicit account of the agent's previous history of action. So long as his previous

principles of general obligation at least as demanding as our principle of minimal altruism. For Hare, the result is utilitarianism. For Gerwirth, the Principle of Generic Consistency yields a variety of principles of general obligation comparable to those discussed here. See, for example, his discussion of "the duty to rescue" in *Reason and Morality*, pp. 217–30. Kohlberg employs "Stage 6" reasoning on behalf of a variety of demanding obligations that must hold according to a "reversibility" requirement where each actor is imagined to trade places with anyone else in the dilemma. See Kohlberg, "Justice as Reversibility," p. 263.

13. For some criticism of the details of this deduction, see part III of my *Tyranny and Legitimacy*. Whether or not we are led to maximin, the situation is constructed so that we have to give special weight to the worst possibilities.

history does not indirectly affect the question by influencing the marginal or global state of an agent at the time of action, it is *entirely* irrelevant to the construction of the problem required by such notions of impartiality. If I must determine my obligations after I have put myself in the place of those who would be affected by my action, a marginal or a global comparison of the results will decide the question (depending on my precise account of impartiality). This notion of the moral point of view leaves no room for any explicit consideration of my *past* history of action.

Yet, from the perspective of the agent considered in isolation, his previous sacrifice does seem to bear on whether his conduct ought to be considered heroic. After all, it is *his* continuous life history. If he performs good deeds which add up in sacrifice to heroic totals, that fact does appear relevant to any assessment of his character and conduct. If individual acts can be considered heroic, in isolation, then there is no reason why the cumulative effects of many actions cannot also be considered heroic. After all, the sacrifices in each case are experienced by the same person. If the limits on moral demands in the basic structure of our common morality make any sense, then they must be applied to a given agent over time taking account of his previous history of action.

It might be objected here that the real point of this argument is that principles of obligation founded in impartiality—such as the principles of general obligation discussed here—conflict with the limits on moral demands that we conventionally assume in our common way of life. The root conflict is thus between impartiality and the limits of conventional morality. What then do "numbers" have to do with it? The impact of numbers—in the sense of enough relevantly similar cases falling under any given principle of general obligation—is to make this theoretical conflict inevitable for any possible principle of general obligation. No matter how trivial the demands of a principle of general obligation, enough similar cases will produce overwhelming demands. With enough numbers, the theoretical vulnerability of these principles becomes a reality. That is the impact of numbers.

It is worth emphasizing that the issue is not merely whether any given principle has an upper limit on required sacrifice. Even when principles explicitly incorporate such limits, repeated applications of the same principle to the same agent produce the same problem once more. Enough repeated applications of marginal sacrifices below any given limit will add up to heroic totals. If I am required, by Rawls's principle of mutual aid, to assist someone "in need or jeopardy provided that one can do so without excessive risk or loss to oneself,"[14] the cumulative occasions for which this principle could be applied by any conscientious moral actor in the real world would overwhelm any reasonable construction of the cutoff for heroism and of the robust sphere of indifference. Each action may be without "excessive risk or loss to onself." Yet, the cumulative effect of consistently applying this principle may be an entire way of life determined by duty and amounting to great sacrifice.

Or consider a principle incorporating a specific limit on sacrifice precisely equal to the cutoff for heroism. Such a principle must either be (1) agent-specific so as to fall outside the category of general obligations or (2) it must be subject to overload problems and hence to breakdown in the basic structure. On the one hand, if the limit were agent-specific, then once a given person had sacrificed his share (as specified by the limit) nothing more could be required of him by the principle. Such a principle would be difficult to defend on grounds of impartiality, as we have seen, since an agent subject to the obligation could not then change places with anyone else (who could perform the action) and leave the

---

14. Rawls, *Theory of Justice*, p. 114.

obligation unchanged. Vulnerability to the obligation would vary depending on the previous history of action of each agent.

On the other hand, if the limit were not agent-specific but were formulated so as to conform to the category of general obligations, then it would be subject to overload problems. Although such a principle could incorporate a limit on sacrifice for any given act or pattern of conduct, recurrent applications of the principle to the same agent would lead, inevitably, to overload. Under a principle of general obligation, the mere fact that one has conformed to a principle (up to the stated limits) in the past does not absolve one from being required to conform to the same principle in the future once again. Successive acts (or patterns of acts) fulfilling any such principle will eventually overload the cutoff for heroism and the robust sphere of indifference. This is why the theoretical vulnerability to overload for principles of general obligation is unavoidable.

Some inventive new principles might also be devised for some of the moral generalization cases. For example, we might imagine an anti-free-rider principle of special obligation—a principle of fairness for accepting benefits. "Anyone who voluntarily accepts the benefits of a general practice is obligated to contribute to it." Such a principle would define special obligations because only those who voluntarily accept the benefits are then required to contribute. We can limit our vulnerability to overload from such a principle by deciding not to accept specific benefits.[15] Although such a principle could be developed to deal with free-rider problems—where the noncontributing agent benefits—it responds only to a small part of our general problem. From an impartial moral perspective, would there not be pressure to

---

15. For an extended discussion of the ambiguities in "accepting benefits" in such a principle of special obligation, see Simmons, *Moral Principles, Political Obligations*, pp. 42–45, 89–90, 138–63, and 187–99.

admit obligations even when an agent does not, himself, benefit from a general practice? Is there not, once more, an impulse to require positive acts on behalf of *any* other person under at least some possible conditions?

I mention the anti-free-rider principle only to show how *special* obligation principles might be directed at some of the particular issues that we often approach more readily with principles of general obligation. It is open to question whether a defensible moral position could be *systematically* constructed out of special obligation principles such as the anti-free-rider and agent-specific formulas. My point is that once principles of *general* rather than special obligation are admitted, the dilemma explored here becomes unavoidable.

Creative efforts at reformulation might, in other words, provide a way out of our dilemma—by providing for new and defensible principles of obligation that were *not* fully general in the manner specified here. Adequate versions of such principles, however, remain to be developed for any systematic response to our dilemma. Some drastic reformulation of our common conceptions is required.

The problem is parallel to that which once faced democratic theory. Just as the notion of democracy was once thought inapplicable to the large-scale nation-state—because large enough numbers made direct democracy impractical—notions of individual responsibility and obligaton require a similarly drastic reformulation at the large scale. The problem facing democratic theory was resolved through the crucial innovation of representation—which permitted democratic institutions to adopt to the large scale. The search for comparable innovations in our notions of individual responsibility and obligation should now be placed high on the agenda of contemporary moral and political theory.

Otherwise, our moral assumptions must require us, as individuals, to take on the full burdens of massive social problems—problems that might better be handled by nation-states and other institutions that can more effectively ensure large-scale social cooperation. In a modern world, instantaneously interconnected by electronic communications and by jet-age transportation, distance no longer insulates us from moral demands arising anywhere in the world.

Our general principles are no longer restricted, by mere happenstance, to those close to us. For we now live in what Marshall McLuhan has called the "global village"[16]—a world in which the mass media may permit *anyone's* problems to be instantaneously brought home to us (literally, to our living rooms). Under these conditions, any plausible principles of general obligation will *routinely* range over so many cases as to overwhelm us—if only we bother to apply those principles to the world.

This argument also has a further implication for *political* theory in that the overload problem exemplifies the incompatibility, at the large scale, of two central components of liberalism: (a) *impartiality* or "equal concern and respect"[17] and (b) *individualism*. Notions of impartiality, as we have seen, press us toward acceptance of general obligations. Notions of individualism require, or implicitly assume, limits on the moral demands that can be made of each individual—limits such as the cutoff for heroism and the robust sphere of indifference. Without such limits, the sphere of negative liberty, where we can be free from interference to do as we please, would lose its value. There would be no realm of permissibly free personal choice, for that part of our life would be

---

16. See, for example, Marshall McLuhan, *War and Peace in the Global Village* (New York: Bantam Books, 1968).

17. For the central place of impartiality or equal concern and respect in contemporary liberal theory, see the discussion of both Rawls and utilitarianism above. In addition, see Ronald Dworkin, *Taking Rights Seriously* (Cambridge, Mass.: Harvard Unversity Press, 1977), pp. 180–83 and 272–78; and for an extended case that a certain kind of impartiality (namely "neutrality") is *the* fundamental assumption of liberalism, see Bruce Ackerman's ambitious new book, *Social Justice in the Liberal State* (New Haven: Yale University Press, 1980), chapter 1.

filled up with moral requirements and overwhelming moral demands.[18]

The conflicts explored here can thus be seen as conflicts between root assumptions of the liberal tradition. I believe that their appeal is wider than liberalism; but the point is that these difficulties pose a challenge that is aimed more squarely at liberalism than at other ideologies and moral positions. To give up *either* the general obligations that are rooted in impartiality or the limits on moral requirements that are presupposed by individualism would represent a very great revision in liberal assumptions as well as in the way most of us think and act with respect to moral questions. Some great revision in our assumptions or in our actions is required. But because I feel genuinely caught in this dilemma myself, I am not now advocating any particular resolution. I have, rather, attempted here to explore systematically the difficulties we face without one.

---

18. See note 1, section 4 for the close connection between negative liberty and these limits on moral demands.

Appendix:
Utilitarianism and Cooperation

In this Appendix, I would like to comment on Donald Regan's newly published *Utilitarianism and Cooperation*.[1] The relevance of Regan's ingenious book is twofold. First, he intends to rebut Lyons's equivalence thesis. Second, he offers a distinctive principle, *Cooperative Utilitarianism*, which can be differentiated from each of the varieties of generalization discussed here.

Regan's argument against Lyons is captured by his recurrent use of this situation in which Whiff and Poof have to decide whether to push or not push a button with payoffs as follows.[2]

		Poof	
		Push	Not-Push
Whiff	Push	10	0
	Not-Push	0	6

If Poof does not push, then act utilitarianism would require Whiff to not-push (since 6 is greater than 0).[3] However, utilitarian generalization, on Regan's interpretation, apparently requires that they both push (since 10 is greater than 6). As Regan says of the situation in which Poof has not pushed:

---

1. Donald Regan, *Utilitarianism and Cooperation* (Oxford: Clarendon Press, 1980).

2. Ibid., pp. 18, 99, 114, 125.

3. Ibid., p. 19.

The consequences of both Whiff and Poof not-pushing are inferior to the consequences of both Whiff and Poof pushing. Therefore, Whiff's not-pushing is not right according to UG' (a principle of utilitarian generalization).[4]

And for a second variant of utilitarian generalization (UG),[5] Regan concludes:

it is clear that UG directs Whiff to push regardless of what Poof does.[6]

Since Whiff must push according to these versions of utilitarian generalization, and since he must not-push according to act utilitarianism, non-equivalence is the result.

I believe that a defender of Lyons's equivalence thesis should claim that Regan is not comparing individual and generalized consequences of the same act under strictly analogous conditions here, for he is comparing the individual consequences of Whiff acting when Poof not-pushes, to the generalized consequences of Whiff acting when Poof pushes. This is how he gets 6 units (for Whiff not-pushing when Poof pushes) compared to 10 units (for Whiff pushing when Poof pushes). Yet, since Poof's not pushing is part of the "complete" description of the individual consequences of Whiff's act, it must also be included in the generalization. An anomoly in this case is that the generalization involves a unit class, since *only* Whiff can produce the consequences of Whiff not-pushing when Poof not-pushes. Hence, I believe

4. Ibid., p. 100. UG' is defined, somewhat tediously, as follows: "An act *a* by an agent Alice is right if and only if the consequences of its being performed by Alice and all other agents who turn out to be similarly situated with Alice if Alice does *a* are at least as good as the consequences of any other available act's being performed by Alice and all other agents who turn out to be similarly situated with Alice if Alice does *a*" (p. 98).

5. UG is defined as follows: "An act is right if and only if the consequences of its being performed by the agent and all other agents similarly situated are at least as good as the consequences of any other available acts being performed by the agent and all other agents similarly situated" (p. 94).

6. Ibid., p. 111.

that if the behavior of others is taken into account, analogously, for individual and generalized consequences, then
nonequivalence does not result.[7]

In any case, Regan's argument that non-equivalence can
result regardless of scale (an argument I think mistaken)
would not affect our claim that non-equivalence comes about
at the large scale, given the cutoff for triviality. It is this claim
which exposes the robust sphere of indifference to the magnification of trivial consequences up to a level of moral significance. The connection between overload and the various
versions of generalization would not, in other words, be affected by Regan's argument.

It is worth noting that Regan's own proposal is vulnerable
to the same two arguments. first, given our cutoff for triviality,
non-equivalence at the large scale would ensue. Second, an
overload of obligations would result from recurrent applications of the principle to any given agent. Regan's own proposal is "cooperative utilitarianism":

> what each agent ought to do is to co-operate, with who-
> ever else is co-operating, in the production of the best
> consequences possible given the behavior of non-
> cooperators.[8]

This injunction is broken down into five steps: (a) an
agent "should hold himself ready to do his part in the best pattern of behavior for the group of cooperators," (b) he should
determine "which of those other agents are available to be
co-operated with," (c) "he should estimate the behavior or
disposition of non-cooperators," (d) "he should identify the
best possible pattern of behavior for the group of co-
operators...given the behavior (or dispositions to behave) of
the non-cooperators," (e) "he should do his part in the best
pattern of behavior just identified."[9]

---

7. See our discussion in section 14 above.
8. Regan, *Utilitarianism and Cooperation*, p. 124.
9. Ibid., pp. 135–36.

This theory can be viewed as combining (1) a version of our actual consequences version of generalization with (2) special requirements about the coordination and encouragement of such general patterns of behavior. As such, it seems susceptible to the same analysis as the one we presented in sections 17 and 18. First, it is possible for a general pattern I am cooperating with to produce aggregate good consequences of great significance even though my contribution is so tiny that it falls below our cutoff for triviality. If the $G = N \times S$ formula is applied to such a general pattern, it is possible for N to be so large that a significant G corresponds to an insignificant S. Regan does not discuss our cutoff for triviality. As a utilitarian, however, he must either (a) accept it and be vulnerable to this point or (b) reject it and accept the moralization of every trivial effect (and hence the collapse of the robust sphere of indifference).

Furthermore, it should be obvious that recurrent applications of this principle would require me to coordinate with an overwhelming number of general patterns producing good consequences. For every such pattern, I must conform to the five steps mentioned above: holding myself ready, estimating the others available to join in, estimating the effects of those who do not join, identifying "the best possible pattern of the group of co-operators" and, lastly, doing my part in the cooperative enterprise. Imagine an agent conscientiously applying these steps to each good cause in the random list of collective efforts mentioned in section 18. If the actual consequence version of generalization leads to overload under those conditions, then so does this proposal.

Index